UTILITIES NEARBY

MUSINGS ON THE OFF-GRID REAL ESTATE SCENE OF SANTA FE, TAOS & NORTHERN NEW MEXICO

By

Jes Márquez

ISBN 978-1-7339209-0-2

1. Sustainable Living 2. Southwest
3. Travel / United States / West / Mountain

Library of Congress Control Number
2019938905

Jes Márquez—
Utilities Nearby

Copyright © 2019 Jes Márquez.
All rights reserved including the right of reproduction in
whole or in part in any form.

Edited by
Christopher Márquez

Published by Species Spectrum LLC
Santa Fe, New Mexico, U.S.A.

Printed in the United States of America
Illustrations, book cover & design by Jes Márquez
© 2019 Jes Márquez. All rights reserved.

For my husband
& the loyal readers of Santa Fe/Taos Craigslist

Author's Note

Right now someone is dreaming about moving to a mesa in northern New Mexico. Around here off the grid properties are astoundingly omnipresent. For several years my post *Caution: Off-Grid Solar Power Renters* has appeared under Craigslist's Santa Fe/Taos rentals. This book, *Utilities Nearby* is a non-fiction account of my anecdotal experiences living off the grid near Santa Fe. It also compiles letters from Craigslist readers who shared their passionate thoughts with me on living (or not living) in northern New Mexico.

People wrote to me because they were sorry they ever moved to New Mexico or because they wanted to come back and were sorry they left. They wrote lamenting about the atrocious rental scene of Santa Fe. They were born and raised Santa Feans, now displaced and people from across the country with a nagging infatuation for adobe homes and sunsets. Santa Fe is an equally wonderful and irksome lover. The New Mexico sun shines on the most spectacular and oddball real estate in the United States—even appearing in the "What You Get" section of *The New York Times* featuring your choice of a half-million dollar colonial home in Connecticut, or a sprawling off-grid Earthship near Taos, New Mexico.

This book is a conversation on the meaning of dwellings, living simply and the American West. For clarity I have corrected grammar and punctuation of readers' feedback in response to my original Craigslist post. For privacy, replies are referenced as anonymous, initials, or first names. Whether my post brought you laughter or disdain, I relished hearing from you.

Utilities Nearby fits perfectly in a nicho for it is a niche in Southwest reading that was under represented until now.

May this book provide you with useful insights into New Mexico's real estate, a "survival guide" if you will. Join me as we scratch beneath the adobe veneer that both enchants and exasperates. There are no guarantees, but upon completion of this book you might be able to convert watts into kilowatt-hours. The only free part is high voltage humor amped with personal experience. *Utilities Nearby* is for everyone near and far who holds a place in their hearts for New Mexico.

Thank you to everyone who has written to me.

Jes Márquez

Albuquerque, NM
March 2019

DISCLAIMER

Any opinions or actions this book inspires are your responsibility and are not the fault, nor the responsibility of the author or publisher. If you thrive and benefit, please send me a kick back.

"You are the kind of pathetic imbecile that will help man take two steps back and zero forward."

Sent from my iPad

-Craigslist reader

CHAPTERS

ZONE 2	11
WINTER OFF THE GRID	22
GLAMPING	54
THE SANTA FE LIFE CYCLE	66
NINE SHADES OF BEIGE	92
THE KEN BURNS WEST EFFECT	105
IN THE DEVELOPING WORLD	119
ENCHANTED ABANDONMENT, DISENCHANTED SUBURBIA	127
UTILITIES NEARBY: RUSTIC RETREAT = VIRTUOUS SOULS	159
WHAT'S HAWAII GOT TO DO WITH IT?	184
THE TAOS HIPPIE REBUTTAL	204
THE LEW WALLACE CURSE OF NEW MEXICO	227
GLOSSARY OF SANTA FE REAL ESTATE TERMS	239
NEIGHBORHOODS OF SANTA FE, NEW MEXICO	242
ORIGINAL CRAIGSLIST POST	250
ACKNOWLEDGEMENTS	259

THE SANTA FE LIFE CYCLE

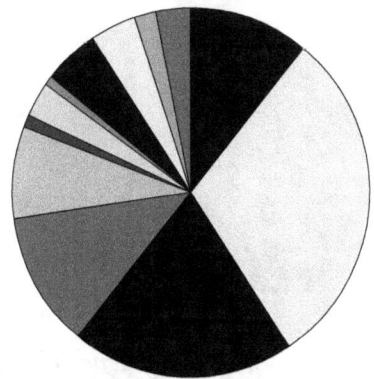

11% Moved Here After Divorce/Break Up

20% Thinking About Chakras, Astrology & Energy Fields

30% Retired/Bored & Joined the Eldorado HOA

12% Looking for a Cheaper Casita

8% La Virgen de Guadalupe

1% The Chile is Too Hot

3% Is that an O'Keeffe?

1% Still Hating Backyard Chickens

5% I Can't Wait to Retire in Santa Fe!

4% Remaining Youth Exodus

2% Dreaming About Going Off-Grid

3% I'm Sorry I Ever Moved Here & Can't Wait to Leave

© Jes Márquez

ZONE 2

"New Mexico…Yeah, I got a friend in San Diego."

-Antique Shop in Virginia

At Santa Fe's Jackalope my friend Carol and I wandered from "Prairie Dog Village" to the blue-rimmed margarita glasses that used to be made in Mexico but are now made in China. This was some years back when Santa Fe was still semi-affordable. Jackalope is a longstanding icon of Santa Fe with imports ranging from terra cotta pots and serapes to pan pipe music. It's a destination to take the kids and out of town guests. Get grandma a taco and park her in front of the prairie dogs while you try on ponchos and buy Nag Champa incense.

Carol has lived in Santa Fe since the early 1980's. Today for no particular reason we perused the postcard section of Jackalope. There it was: "New Mexico" scrawled in bold letters across a hot orange sunset with a big fat saguaro cactus. Carol was irate. She took the postcard to the clerk and pointed, "This isn't New Mexico. See that? That cactus doesn't grow here. This sunset happened in Arizona." Carol was like a detective on the trail of facts. She tapped the photo for emphasis. The clerk understood, but it didn't

Utilities Nearby

matter because tourists didn't care about the truth. People in khaki shorts were still buying fake Santa Fe souvenirs.

There are no saguaro cacti in New Mexico. This lack of knowledge amongst some Land of Enchantment seekers is a cherished New Mexican pet peeve. It's as notorious as *New Mexico Magazine's* feature, "One of our Fifty is Missing" where fans of the state share what it's like when outsiders don't know we are part of the United States. Look to the Sonoran Desert several hundred miles into Arizona if you want the cartoon desert experience. New Mexico is the land of juniper trees, high mountain deserts, tumbleweeds and sharp goat head thorns that poke holes in bike tires and bare feet. We have cholla and ocotillo cacti that are more diverse than the plant life of social media emojis.

Recently my friend Darryl, who is from the other side of the world, wrote to me: "Jes, how hard is it to get into New Mexico?" His choice of a Mexican flag emoji was hopeful, as if New Mexico was a Bermuda triangle in the desert, the last safe haven for those who were declined USA green cards. It reminded me of one of New Mexico's favorite bumper stickers, "It's Not New and it's Not Mexico." Such sentiment was nearly as popular as the heyday of "Visualize Whirled Peas." Keep your eyes open when following an ancient Subaru and you might spot one of these infamous bumper stickers.

New Mexico is a place both forgotten and treasured. An old acquaintance in Chicago assumes New Mexico celebrates, "Year around tank top weather." To people "Back East" New Mexico is that mystical area toward California but closer to the imaginary border of Arizona and Texas. It's a land of nicer weather and better food. There are misconceptions, myths and legends when it comes to the Land of Enchantment, but the most dazzling of all is the legion of real estate listings for off-grid properties.

I've held a fascination with real estate from a young age. My family moved to New Mexico when I was eleven years old. It was the height of Nickelodeon's *Hey Dude*, the show about teenagers living on a ranch in the real Sonoran Desert where the saguaros grow. This show seemed authentic because it wasn't filmed on a back alley soundstage and the "killer cacti" weren't made of plastic. The bouncy *Hey Dude* theme song ran through my head while my parents looked at houses and I gleefully imagined that I would finally get a horse. My parents eventually bought a house on the outskirts of Santa Fe, but my *Hey Dude* anthem failed to manifest a horse.

Santa Fe, sometimes referenced as "Adobe Disneyland," is largely the destination of retirees and artists. It's a quiet place to be a teenager and everyone in the yoga class is typically a lot older, but some of my best friends are baby boomers. As a teenager in Santa Fe I spent time at The Ark, a bookstore on Romero Street. It's the new age stalwart of local bookstores long outlasting Borders Books, Sanbusco Shopping Center and the onslaught of Amazon.

The Ark existed before the Santa Fe Railyard qualified as a "District." In the old days the Railyard was a huge lumpy dirt parking lot for Santa Feans driving old Subarus and the parking was always free. Locals could still walk to the plaza without paying a dime. Rabid meter maids were easy to avoid or the city couldn't afford to employ many of them. Free parking was one of the desirable perks of not living in a crowded urban sprawl maze like California. This was before Santa Fe decided it needed it's own REI outdoor store, even though Albuquerque already had an REI. It was before the Railyard invasion of "West Coast Industrial Chic," a rebellion against four centuries of "Santa Fe Tan."

By the way, the specifics on "Santa Fe Tan" are best defined by the Historic Preservation Division. Some pockets of Santa Fe are rebelling with cargo container buildings and others are devout adobe enthusiasts. Basically, after allowing a Super Walmart and a beige Target store on the south side,

Utilities Nearby

it's really important that we preserve the original character of Canyon Road and the area surrounding the Santa Fe Plaza. This historic radius extends from the pink fajita cart on the southwest corner of the Plaza to Paseo de Peralta.

In my teenage years at The Ark bookstore I could be found beyond the Astrology and the "What-am-I-eating-and-doing-with-my-life-section." Ensconced in the house and architecture books, I fantasized about having my own house in New Mexico. It would be a place far from town where I could have a horse and a pack of dogs like other eccentrics who preferred nature to people. I frolicked in coffee table book escapism; one featuring Ten Thousand Waves, the local and world-renowned Japanese Spa that used to be less crowded before Oprah mentioned it.

Somewhere between photos of tranquil wooden hot tubs nestled in the forests and crude diagrams on how to use chicken wire to build a strawbale wall, I decided living off the grid would be the opportunity of a lifetime. It was my dream to be self-sufficient while maintaining a semi-cosmopolitan outlook.

After all, I was fortunate enough to grow up in sunny New Mexico, or "Zone 2" as referenced by the solar companies. Each solar Zone is defined as insolation, meaning energy of the sun's rays in any given area. Compared with more northern latitudes such as Zone 6 (Seattle), or Zone 5 (Maine), New Mexico is a solar power Eden. Zone 2 is obviously only surpassed by Zone 1, which is a small oblong circle encompassing the electricity loving Las Vegas Strip and the scorching heat of Death Valley. I should note that nearby Furnace Creek, California holds the hottest temperature ever recorded on earth at 134 °F. Las Vegas, Nevada has an annual high temperature of 80 °F mitigated by deep freeze air conditioning inside the casinos, swimming pools full of dolphins and hanging out with Wayne Newton. Zone 1 is clearly the lucrative location for the air conditioner repairman.

New Mexico averages over three hundred days of sunshine each year. We were the original "Sunshine State" before losing that slogan to Florida in 1934. By the time Anita Bryant was introduced in 1969 as the spokeswoman for Florida orange juice campaigns, "The Citrus State" was a slogan relic of Florida's past. It was now all about drinking "Sunshine." Back then New Mexico wasn't privy to copyright laws usurping a no paper work Gentleman's Agreement between the States. The "Land of Enchantment" wasn't officially adopted until 1999! Since the Burmese Python invasion of the Everglades National Park, Florida might benefit from a new slogan and could easily return the "Sunshine State" to sunnier, python-free New Mexico. Perhaps Florida could re-brand with something like "The State Invasive Species Love Most." In the meantime have fun hunting for New Mexico's vintage Sunshine State souvenirs.

Harnessing the power of the sun seemed like a plausible dream in New Mexico. In my mind people who lived off the grid were the true self-starters. They didn't care about convenience stores or gated communities or good school districts. They were the kind of people that loathe Home Owner's Associations. Retiring to a condo in Florida would be insanity. People who sought a life off the grid were wilderness seekers like me.

My earliest memories are of mountains, camping and wild places. Experiencing hiking trails as a little kid had a major impact on my lifelong love of the outdoors. Although backcountry survival or home building was not my dad's forte, he dutifully staked down the family Eureka tent during high winds. Given a choice, my dad prefers staying at three star hotels to camping. The lure of a clean hotel room, continental breakfast, complimentary copies of USA Today and HBO beckons some more than others.

My parents never spent their weekends building a deck or turning old wood pallets into Adirondack chairs. In-

Utilities Nearby

stead my mother was a passive witness to T.V. home shows, "Doesn't that look nice? Look at the before and after! I'd love landscaping like that!" my mother would say. The T.V. dramatically panned to what was just a dirt yard a few hours earlier. Now it was a lush tropical oasis complete with a movie projector, koi fishpond and a built in BBQ pit. The episode ended at dusk with a family enjoying their new backyard, roasting marshmallows and inviting friends over for a private screening of a Disney classic. The same vicarious living happens in the pages of *Sunset Magazine*.

I came from a family who couldn't assemble a desk from IKEA. What appeared to be four wooden legs and screws was in actuality an arduous cuss and complain affair that would take several hours. The instructions that came with the desk stated that just one Allen wrench was required for assembly. Unfortunately, no one in my family could find an Allen wrench in the mangled nuts and bolts toolbox. Years later after convoluted particleboard desks were thrown in the trash, someone would finally find the missing Allen wrench.

These people couldn't possibly be my true family. I had a knack for design as well as basic common sense that didn't mean fixing the family refrigerator shelf with half a roll of duct tape or using channel locks on the bathroom faucet when the knob fell off. It seemed impossible that both my parents had graduate degrees. I was enamored by the do-it-yourself folks before "DIY" was an in vogue acronym. DIY people built porches, in-law suites and renovated chef kitchens. The DIY crowd were the people who had drills and hammers in their hands on early Saturday mornings. I like people who can fix and flip a house without breaking a sweat, the kind of people who buy raw land and turn it into paradise.

To out of state relatives we were the weird family "from New Mexico" who lived in an authentic early 1980's passive solar house with a woodstove, brick floors and those huge south facing windows that get cloudy and trap moisture after a few years. Twice we had a bullsnake in the house. Bullsnakes are not poisonous so we simply opened the door and let the snake slither back outside. Our house always had a few mice that were gung-ho on procreating. It was a true New Mexico house without air conditioning or even a swamp cooler because, "It doesn't get hot in northern New Mexico" (or if it does, it didn't used to get hot in northern New Mexico), or it's El Niño or La Niña or Global Warming. Overall the house maintained a comfortable temperature most of the year with an accurate south facing orientation.

My cousins lived in normal houses in Texas ranch homes with central air, beige carpet and floral wallpaper. They bought home décor at TJ MAXX that wasn't even collectible. They did sacrilegious things like frequenting mainstream movie theaters and eating at chain restaurants. My cousins decorated their home for Halloween and lived in cookie-cutter neighborhoods where everyone had cute kids that trick-o-treated in store bought costumes. When we visited Texas, my cousins wondered why I wore fleece vests and had clothes that were "poop brown" instead of pink or purple. Maybe it was because in my world all the houses were brown and the landscape was mostly brown too.

Friends from Arizona always visited Santa Fe in the summer. They never thought it was hot in Santa Fe, but back home they had a colossal air conditioner. Even if they drove a black car in Phoenix it didn't matter because their house was kept at the same temperature as their refrigerator. Deep freeze air conditioning like that makes me feel guilty for pulling a comforter over me while a heat wave rages outside for nights and days on end.

In college I had an instructor who built an off the grid home in New Mexico. This furthered my fascination with the real possibilities of living off-grid. In a part of Santa Fe County known for having a high-density rattlesnake population, my instructor had managed to build a self-sufficient adobe house from scratch. He actually had a family and wasn't a solitary hermit hiding out in the desert. When I toured the house, it reminded me that my house dreams were achievable.

Around the same time, I came across a book called Arctic Homestead (2000) by Norma Cobb. I read it in the University of New Mexico's Student Union Building oblivious to some fraternity streakers gallivanting through the food court. These streakers were hardly planning futures beyond keggers and lunch at Chick-Fil-A. I was planning a homestead. What mattered to me was that I was born too late to get an Alaskan land claim prior to 1986. The era of homesteading was over by the time I was out of diapers. This conjured up envy in me toward those lucky old farts who were given the opportunity to hand hewn logs and melt snow on a woodstove.

The Cobb family managed to settle a land parcel and erect a cozy cabin right in the middle of Alaska's long dark winters. They could mush husky dogs and watch the northern lights in absolute pristine quiet. By comparison, my foray into off the grid life in sunny Northern New Mexico would be easy. The world was already decades into more efficient solar technology. A sunny location coupled with cheaper photovoltaic systems meant off the grid living would be a cakewalk in sunglasses.

For a period of my young adulthood, I'll admit publicly right now that I was captivated by yurts. The traditional nomadic homes of the Mongols are insulated with several layers of thick felted wool from an actual sheep or yak. No need for pink cotton candy insulation made of fiberglass that may or may not pose a health risk other than skin irritation and cancer. The ancient Mongols got natural home building right the first time. These circular structures draw in the New Mexico crowd alongside Tibetan prayer flags. I hope my Craigslist reader, Sponge-Bath-Yurt-Guy-

North-of-Taos, reads this and sees that we have something in common.

While I'm not a big fan of perpetual sponge baths, I am a proponent of yurts. At the time of my yurt infatuation I still believed in astrology, Mercury retrograde, the law of attraction and Emotional Freedom Taping (EFT). This was due to over exposure to Santa Fe during pivotal years of my youth. Astrology doesn't necessarily relate to housing, but I'll bet money that just about anyone contemplating yurt living in New Mexico has dabbled in astrology. Such would-be astrologers also play Native American flutes badly and some of these people still wear Vibram 5Fingers (Yeah, so did I).

Santa Feans like to go out for indie films at the Jean Cocteau, The Screen and CCA because it would be uncultured to be caught in a mainstream movie theater. Thanks to George R.R. Martin the Jean Cocteau is still open. While The Screen teetered on life support for a while, it's where I saw The Cave of the Yellow Dog (2005), a Mongolian film that further instilled my attraction to yurt living. On the remote wind swept open lands of Mongolia I could see how a real felted yurt made a home for a family of four. Although I couldn't imagine sharing my personal yurt space with three family members (at least not mine), the cozy appearance and nomadic quiet captivated me. The Mongolian family's yurt was still far roomier than the craze of tiny houses sweeping America today.

In my youth I was a pet sitter around Santa Fe; I lived out of a duffle bag in other people's homes with other people stuff and other people pets. This was long before pet sitting became a sought after Santa Fe profession by the semi-retired. It was considered the ideal position for a young person attempting to hack it in Santa Fe with a liberal arts degree and a self-employment dream that wasn't chump. During those years I slept with a lot of dogs and lived in many homes around Santa Fe. I saw how people lived. I drove to houses accessed by roads that went through arroyos. In the winter, I bounced down slushy pot holed single lane roads through the trees of Glorieta. This required gunning my Subaru to get momentum where the road quickly rose uphill then dropped down to a driveway that dashed to the right. There I arrived at a cabin with two exuberant dogs and a heater out of propane.

I always welcomed the home out of town. The sheer vertical road leading to the house of the ancient wolf dog always had a touch of treachery, but with firm acceleration and the sense that leaning forward helped my car get to this mountain retreat, I could pretend to be home here. It was far preferable compared with the house on the paved road where walking dogs meant being immersed in urban adobe sprawl. So what if the convenience of De Vargas Center was a five-minute walk or drive! Neighborhoods had rules. I was one of those people that hated being told what to do. It was just a reminder of how off the grid living was for people like me. I wanted a home of my own, not too different than the anarchists interested in turning an island hideaway into a new sovereign nation.

Out of a desire to rekindle a simpler life, off the grid welcomed just about anyone with the DIY loving arms of self-sufficiency. I had read about the hippies who built tree houses in northern California in the 1970's, how their kids grew up barefoot and the amazing things that could be achieved with a golf cart battery. Golf cart batteries were amongst the early relics of solar energy pioneers. On dusty trails, powered only by the bipedal motion of my bicycle and a pair of wild border collies, I noted how large swaths of land in Santa Fe County are actually off-grid. Never mind the proximity to a state capital, just out of town, acres upon acres of off-grid paradise surrounded me.

Propelled by my convictions and supposed due diligence, it was my husband who happened upon our almost dream home. For a long time I'd waxed on about how one day we would leave the grid forever and never look back.

My husband trusted me and this rural off the grid rental home we had stumbled upon was a loving attempt to please me and the dogs. I'll be honest, for all the reading I had done about planet earth loving folks standing barefoot in the mud, building hornos, permaculture communities and Scandinavian chalets in the back country, I didn't confirm that much before my husband and I signed a lease on an off-grid house that "looked okay" and had "beautiful views." How could anything go wrong when we lived in sunny Zone 2?

WINTER OFF THE GRID

"Never take no cut offs and hurry along as fast as you can."
-Virginia Reed, Donner Party Survivor, 1846

"This home is completely self-sufficient and makes its own electricity."
-Santa Fe County Real Estate Listing

We signed the lease for the solar powered house with "solitude and beautiful vistas." Driving down the winding dirt lane we arrived at our new country home with acres to explore. The dogs were thrilled and so were we. Having lived in New Mexico since I was a kid you would have pegged me as familiar with casita jargon. Normally I would have felt the faint chill or the proverbial red flag in the property description, "Energy conscientious" and quickly moved on. But the allure of an affordable, dog friendly rental wedged against the backdrop of the wilderness made for a hasty marriage into off the grid living.

There are life hacks, comfort hacks and theoretical hacks. Life hacks usually involve things such as putting an egg at the bottom of a flowerpot for healthy plants or using Coca Cola to clean car parts. Comfort hacks involve bagel slicers and things from the Bed, Bath & Beyond store.

Theoretical hacks involve building a fire with two sticks and tearing the foam out of your car seats to make mukluks when your truck breaks down in a remote place during a snowstorm.

    Theoretical hacks are the ones that might save your life. The rest are merely online content creation to impress your friends and sell advertisements. Brands adore catering to the façade of the extreme adventure lifestyle. Using an empty Tic Tac box to hold your smoked paprika on a camping trip is a good example. My husband and mother-in-law both love jackets, coats, containers and kitchen gadgets. Many of my husband's kitchen gadgets fit right in between our zest for "outdoor survival skills" and "luxury cave man." I should mention that most of our practice in "outdoor survival skills" relates to studying You Tube videos of people camping in subzero temperatures while we lay in bed beneath a down comforter.

    We had plenty of life hacks mastered; the vintage stainless steel garlic press, the grapefruit spoon, candle wax to waterproof any standard strike-on-box matches, how to use a tampon as a water filter, how to use a bottle of vodka to dislodge a python latched to your arm, how to turn a tube of lip balm into a mini torch, ten ways a contractor garbage bag and a roll of duct tape can save your life.

    I came across a copy of the US Army Survival Manual belonging to my grandma. She had placed one of those patriotic address sticker labels inside the front cover. Often, my grandma would also stuff old newspaper clippings inside her books with articles about victims of bears, sharks, mountain lions and burglars. Grandma's copy of the US Army Survival Manual proved more useful than the bibles that the Jehovah's witnesses used to bring to my front door. Now my husband and I lived beyond solicitors in a remote enclave of wilderness. Our front door no longer needed my handmade sign that read, "Absolutely No Solicitors." In my US Army Survival Manual, I was reading and wondering

Utilities Nearby

about things Grandma must have wondered about: Could I tie a snare trap? Could I make a bed in a swamp?

Like many people who delve passionately into an alternative lifestyle, my husband and would learn through total immersion. This strategy works for learning a foreign language so it would work for us too. The first thing we learned was that not all solar photovoltaic systems are created equal. This is a critical key point when kicking the proverbial tires of a handful of solar panels on a rustic property and saying, "Yep, looks like there's power." Some solar systems are so hobbled and sun baked that their presence merely implies electricity. Such photovoltaic systems are positioned on broken wood palettes where the sun shines briefly in summer and hardly at all in the winter. Since winter arrives with consistent regularity throughout our lives, this is where the seasonal dip in power will make or break the off-grid dreamer. We soon found out the hard way.

Some wanderer types love to talk about freedom and how free life can be. These are the sorts of people who take photographs of their laptops in scenic locations, like motel swimming pools and the patio at Starbucks. People rattle on about how fortunate they are that they work from home or remotely or how they are a "digital nomad." The paradox is that living "for free" still requires remedial skills in math. Basic arithmetic is a pre-requisite for living off the grid. It's fine to flip the bird at society and say you're getting the hell out of consumer life, but you're still going to do math and you'll still need to buy or trade things from time to time. For every person that has the time to post glitter and allure on social media, someone else is actually just doing it.

Calm down, I'm talking about middle school math. For today's kids who come out of the womb holding their first smart phone this should be easy. Any intelligent person should first learn how to convert the wattage of a solar panel into kilowatt-hours (kWh) before leaping at, "Don't make this your home!" Just like starting a business, there are hidden expenses in adopting any supposed "free" lifestyle. Land, adobe bricks, firewood, woodstoves, plane tickets, vans, fuel, yoga pants and insurance are just the beginning. If you're the anarchist who doesn't need insurance, you'll still need quite a few supplies to survive, even with a rustic set up.

On the topic of insurance, it's the reason we didn't have a woodstove in the strawbale home we rented. When you rent from an on the cheap landlord named Medusa there's not only zero maintenance on your rental property, Medusa will also deny tenants the only rational way to heat an off-grid home—a woodstove. The insurance companies aren't too enthusiastic about having renters with flaming logs inside a house made of straw. What sane person wants to pay more premiums to the insurance company for something that might never happen? This is particularly true when landlords don't trust tenants and vice versa. Toss in a whimsical, organic New Mexico built by hand home that may or may not meet basic inspection and insurance companies say, "Perceived stupidity is costly." Sure, no one likes inspector guy showing up with a clipboard and a lot of criticism concerning your rickety dreams.

Not dealing with building codes or being tied to a hefty mortgage are supposed to be the perks of renting rather than owning. As a renter it's easy to sweep these points under a giant Persian rug. In less than a month, my over educated and under paid spouse and I were moving out of a centrally located half above ground basement Adobe with one window and into the expansive world of off-grid living "just minutes from the Santa Fe plaza." Driving the bumpy dirt road to our new place, summer sunlight on the foothills quickly turned to a monsoon shower. It was a local move and our mandatory high clearance 4WD vehicles were the perfect match for an affordable move into the Santa Fe area rental of our dreams.

Utilities Nearby

I squashed down the dreary feeling of the house when we first looked at the home with the landlord. Perhaps it was nothing more than the gray of an overcast day, the kind of days I love in New Mexico. Now clouds would mean it was time to conserve electricity, instead of watching a movie. Before signing the lease, Medusa the landlord joked about idiots living on the grid. When they have power outages we'd be the ones laughing after the next nor'easter struck New York. In the end we weren't laughing because we couldn't flip on a light switch either.

The day we moved in it was pouring rain. If my "New Ager" fuse hadn't permanently blown out, I would have surmised rain was an omen of renewal instead of a premonition of pending doom. We'd moved a handful of boxes into the rustic kitchen before the crack of thunder clapped its hands at our pathetic lives. The rain began splattering in endless buckets. Living off-grid we were now entwined with nature. Out here not even a thermostat could save us, but I could endure rain better than Oregonians that sold out for sunnier New Mexico. My dream of living at the far edges of humanity in majestic natural splendor had come true.

Beware the absentee out of state landlord who plans to hack it using the previous tenant as the liaison to the new tenant. During the unusual torrential downpour our friendly previous tenant handed us the house keys and didn't say much. There was no hint that we were taking possession to turn key hell. I didn't blame the last tenant for gunning it down the dirt road and not looking back. In survival mode you save yourself, put on the oxygen mask, hug the seat cushion, give away the keys and drive away. Writing out your rent check while you freeze your ass off in the mountains was just the beginning of imagining moving into one of the nice hotels in Santa Fe.

Forget wasting money on that whole property management company thing or all that hassle providing blood samples, invasive background checks and admitting your dog weighs over thirty pounds. Feel the hair on your neck rise when the rental agreement asks for astrological information. Sometimes people are simply devoid of an ethical conscience regardless of their sun sign and no amount of astrological analysis is going to dim the lights on new age charlatans. However, know that your answer determines whether or not you'll get back your deposit.

Even with the advent of Yelp, Trip Advisor and Craigslist people occasionally unknowingly buy snake oil. A couple years later we ran into the previous tenant who thought we looked familiar. That's when we all entered memory flashback, "The house from hell!" Right then and there we shared a joyous conversation of shared experience followed by the shock that the same Medusa landlord was still on the loose. We finally understood the respiratory health problems all of us encountered living in the house and the wicked chill we felt on that convenient six-month lease. We were just relieved it was all over and shared a hemp milk wheat grass concoction favored by the elite with first world problems.

When you go to the movies in Santa Fe you're probably sitting next to someone that once rented the same house you are currently living in. For years I have watched the same Craigslist rentals posted with a suspiciously high rotation. Some of these properties involve reduced rent for animal care or being vegan. Lots of folks are the non-committal type and that's why some love the six-month lease. Clearly something is dreadfully wrong with the "Visionary Artist Retreat" that keeps popping up for rent.

Any renter who is not desperate for a dog friendly, affordable property within fifty miles of Santa Fe would ask the self-proclaimed off-grid builder/landlord, "Is this the first and only home you have ever built?" Does said landlord currently live in another (better built) self-built off-grid home? I might be the only one who notices that the hip-

Utilities Nearby

pie solar loving landlord either lives tucked away with grid power in a home they didn't build or in a house that doesn't suffer the mistakes of the one you're about to rent. This first self-built solar loving "oops baby" is still a cash cow for the plucky wanna-be Santa Fe/Taos county landlord.

The luckiest landlords have two off-grid homes to rent on the same property. I will call this genius of real estate investing "a guest house/studio." In our case, we rented what was dubbed the "main house" implying that we were the privileged renters of a hacienda compound. The "guesthouse" was rented out to someone far more spiritual than us who read Siddhartha and slept in a hammock. Despite our differences we all shared a few things in common: We had virtually no electricity, no woodstove and spent most of our money on propane, but we're still freezing. However, the guesthouse was clearly newer built and positioned on a slightly sunnier portion of the property. But with just three solar panels and tired batteries, even the would be lone monk was having trouble adapting.

It's rare to see property listings clarify stats on the capacity of homegrown electricity. Vagueness trumps disclosure with, "Hey, check out the sunset!" Off the grid landlords are eager to get their hovels rented, especially in the spring. Six-month leases are born because many properties are three season homes at best. Only once have I witnessed a landlord honestly state such awareness concerning their woodsy mountain retreat. Tenants tend to be miffed after six-months of overpriced camper style living and start packing up. This is when landlords reload their mousetrap, "Low Carbon Footprint Artist Retreat Available for Rent."

In the beginning, our six-month lease still meant it was time for me to have a big sofa. My friend gave me the sofa I'd always wanted so that I could finally enjoy delayed adulthood by having a real living room. Another friend loaned me her small pick up truck so I could move my behemoth sofa that was far less mobile than a futon. I was like a bird pulling out my chest feathers to make way for a cozy nest and my first real house. My husband and I now enjoyed his and hers closets even if we had to forego electricity. The dogs trotted happily in and out of the house pleased with the freedom of their new rural lifestyle.

Our off the grid home was paradoxically confusing. The presence of power outlets does not necessarily translate to having electricity. There was a plethora of electric sockets and ceiling fans, which could never be used. The house had enough storage space to please sentimental packrats and organizational freaks, but we soon experienced a dearth of power even for souls who had made a concerted effort to conserve what sunlight delivered. No longer would we plug in our handy digital alarm clock that projected the time off the ceiling with a snazzy red glow. This was either a comfort hack or just plain lazy because we never had to strain our necks in the middle of the night. But living off the grid, time no longer mattered.

The most important part about living off the grid reminded me of the movie Gremlins. In the same way you never feed a gremlin after midnight, you never (read rarely) use a heat source appliance off the grid. The obvious part of this mess happens in the kitchen, where a blender might be okay, but a toaster oven is a no go. Getting rid of the electric waffle iron was no big deal. It's the sort of useless kitchen appliance that ends up on the shelves of Goodwill right next to the Quesadilla Maker, the George Foreman Grill, Billy Bass the Talking Fish, kitchen stuff made by Ron Popeil, QVC specials, and the deluge of old coffee pots. No sane person actually needs any of these things. In the end, life is still complicated and the turkey cooker was a pain in the ass to clean anyway.

Diving passionately into off the grid living requires compromise, adaptation and changes to everyday parts of life. How you make coffee is a simple example of a first world problem with too many options. I have a friend who religiously preps her coffee pot before going to bed. This way she can stumble out of bed, trip over the cat and navigate to the on button. Coffee pots weren't my thing as I was a preacher of the sublime French Press. Pioneers never needed electricity and neither did I! If I really needed an espresso there was the Italian stovetop steamer that didn't require electricity. Like #vanlife we erroneously assumed that we only needed to power a laptop, cell phone and the internet. Everything else was extraneous, at least until the first snowfall. Deceptively, for brief moments it's as if all of life really can be broken down into a HuffPost 5 Things/7 Reasons/10 Places article.

Coincidentally, just prior to moving off the grid my mother-in-law had given me a cappuccino machine. It was sleek, shiny, spared no expense crème-de-la-crème. My cappuccino machine came with all the accoutrements: Single, double, the mini pod, the milk steamer cleaner pin, the little brush and most importantly, the double ended tapper to smooth the top of perfectly brewed espresso. All of this fit neatly tucked away beneath the water supply. Then there was the power cord. One press of a button and the machine heated up quickly with a blinking light alerting me that my espresso was ready to brew.

This was a fancy gadget in my life. Previously, French Press simplicity had been my self-righteous coffee. I was now a coffee snob who professed how espresso grinds should have the texture of beach sand. Though it took time, I eventually mastered the art of enviable frothed milk. This skill set relied upon electricity. Flimsy battery operated milk frothers couldn't possibly replace the once in a lifetime expensive gift of electric cappuccino machine. Rarely in my adult life, had I ever had my own kitchen.

Living exclusively solar bound means no grid tie in. We were adapting to a life without heat source appliances. At first blush, most small appliances were plain ridiculous components of western energy hogging civilization. I could count on one hand the number of times in my life that I had used a hairdryer. No one actually used heated paraffin wax footbaths except the day they bought it. After that it went into a closet because it was so much of a hassle to set up in the first place. Who actually uses a curling iron in Santa Fe? I felt smugness in telling Medusa landlord that I never needed a hair dryer or an electric waffle iron.

I pulled out our vintage Italian stovetop espresso maker. My cappuccino machine was an electricity offender, but I didn't want to get rid of my stainless beauty. It had given me a sense of home. The sound of it brewing comforted me on cold mornings, like the bustle and brewing sounds of the original Santa Fe Baking Company, back when Mary Charlotte sat in the corner everyday. (Kindly spare me the seething letter about how cappuccino machines are incompatible with off the grid philosophy).

Yes, I might sound like the vegan that can't give up a love of fur coats. Diabolically opposed elements are often parts of the human psyche. At least one off-gridder wrote to me and declared that her cappuccino machine "worked just fine" in her off the grid home. Why she was perusing Craigslist Santa Fe/Taos rentals when she was purportedly already living the sweet off-grid life was another question. This same individual also touted that she had, "Never run out of power." Such holy tread lightly carbon foot print preachers will conveniently omit the stats on their sun loving energy system. This omission is due to the supposed individuality of each off-grid person. It's like a discussion about birth control or alcohol tolerance until it's mutually agreed, "Well, everyone's body is different." Living off-grid it's easy to gloss over the merits without divulging the major pit falls, the learning curves or the times of self-doubt.

Our kitchen was rustic and large. A herd of mice lived in the oven migrating through the cabinetry. My cappuccino machine sat unplugged on the counter. On sunny mornings, I looked at the inverter and things seemed to be

Utilities Nearby

okay so I quickly prepared an espresso, turning the machine on for five minutes, brewing and steaming my milk in rapid succession. Then I mindfully and immediately pulled the plug, because even idle plugged in appliances suck a little electricity. Before winter we sat outside drinking coffee looking at the isolated beautiful vistas as if we were the luckiest people on earth.

On sunny days we did the occasional load of laundry in the fragile off-grid washer with a load capacity of one t-shirt and four pairs of underwear. For a brief time I thought we were doing a commendable job of unplugging things and looking up at the sky for the daily forecast. The sight of monsoon clouds meant hurry up and power down. Hanging my clothes out on the line with the dramatic backdrop of nature reminded me of films about middle-aged American women who move to Italy seeking plates of pasta and an epiphany on what life really means.

We were achieving success in our off-grid life. The internet worked okay and the laptops were kept charged. It was part of that "working from home" thing which accounts for everyone in Santa Fe County that doesn't work for the State. We virtually eliminated our use of lamps and opted for LED string lights in our bedroom and kitchen. Every light bulb was of minimal wattage and was turned on for minimal amounts of time. Neither my husband nor I paid a lot of attention to the monolithic propane heater that sat waiting to disappoint us when old man winter arrived.

By October I noticed how it was often colder in the house than it was outside. I started wearing my jacket indoors all the time, even in bed. Days were shorter. The sun dipped earlier behind the canyon and the house got darker. The same doors that had flung open to the expansive views during the summer months were now drafty. An icy bitterness seeped through the cracks and there was the distant eerie heckle of Medusa the landlord that had just devoured her next victims.

To lift morale I plugged in my cappuccino machine. The day prior had been sunny. The espresso was ready. I was frothing the milk when the steam suddenly waned, strained and stalled. We were out of power. It was no different than the very occasional on grid power outages where there is an abrupt monastic stillness because Netflix lost connection and the dishwasher stopped mid-cycle. Devices ask questions about what other networks might be available. One realizes just how noisy a quiet plugged in house can be when the hum of electricity ceases. The utter solitude of hearing oneself chew granola while a pine needle floats to the ground are perks of the off-grid lifestyle. Some folks thrive and others lose their minds.

The oblivious heathens living on the grid freak out when a power outage occurs at night. "Who has a flashlight?" is followed by the realization that there's ice cream in the freezer that could melt before being eaten. Some people are organized enough to keep a plethora of flashlights with fresh batteries in a neat little basket by the front door. I used to envy such people so I married one. Growing up my family either couldn't find a flashlight and cussed while stumbling through the dark or when they finally did find a flashlight, the batteries were dead so they would cuss some more. By that time the power grid had been restored, well in advance of melting ice cream.

The biggest difference for the off-gridder vs. on-gridder is that typically after a few hours in silence, the sound of power returns in full force for the on-gridder. Living off-grid means hoping the next day will be sunny so that the batteries can recharge over the next twenty-four hours. Even the holiest energy conscientious folks will experience a power outage, despite impenetrable smugness. True off-gridders laugh about running out of power like the friendly neighbor a few doors down from our hovel. I couldn't help noticing that our friendly neighbor had fancy, new looking photovoltaic solar panels that repositioned themselves to the sun, like the leaves of a plant. Our panels by comparison looked like they were purchased in the 1970's. Some abandoned panels were dumped in a field as we soon discovered on our walks around the property.

By November we had already unplugged our small refrigerator to mitigate the number of power outages that were coming faster as winter approached. Medusa the landlord could have installed a more costly yet more efficient propane refrigerator, but we weren't that lucky. Cutting corners means buying a tiny standard refrigerator that will eat your solar energy rather than investing in available alternatives in synch with the sans utilities philosophy. Take a gander at off-grid appliances and you'll see what I mean. They do exist, but they cost a precious penny.

The first snowstorm arrived in November engulfing the solar panels until my jaunts outside with the snow broom. Unlike mucking a horse stall, it's important to be attentive to avoid scratching the panels. The juniper trees dotting our property sagged with an unusually heavy snowfall. At other times in my life I have welcomed the white blanket of quiet cold beauty. In a Hallmark Christmas movie our home would have radiated the warmth of a glowing fire and hot cocoa after a family sojourn of cross-country skiing. With a can of whipped cream and marshmallows in hand, I would have worn a red turtleneck and my husband, a green turtleneck—like picturesque New Englanders. The epic feeling of living in a snowy wilderness faded in the off-grid house with no cozy fireplace or woodstove. I lamented about how just about every one of those backcountry hut-to-hut ski cabins have a woodstove, maybe even a fireplace. We had neither.

Our dank kitchen stove sat against the rodent occupied interior wall far from daylight. I stared into my homemade green pea soup bubbling like a murky geyser and chopped carrots by light of my headlamp. This wasn't Everest base camp. In a normal home I might have been wearing one of those fuzzy robes. Yeah, what a wimp! Out here I was wearing snow boots, fleece pants, beanie cap, hoodie and a ski jacket while stirring my pea soup with a vintage wooden spoon.

We looked unkempt not just on Saturdays, but all the time. My husband quit shaving because the bathroom was so cold. His face became scrubby. He wore a hat to bed, like you might do when you're a hardcore winter camper or when you rent an off-grid house without a heat source in the mountains. I remembered our old life in Santa Fe when my husband looked professional and when every once in a while, I wore a skirt and put on mascara.

Proactive people under freezing circumstances could have purchased a couple space heaters while muttering under their breath about the inconsiderate landlord. Such a simple dream of an electric heat dish was beyond the reach of our off-grid home. One the challenges in off-grid adaptation is the difficulty of providing continuous power to any appliance that uses heat, such as a space heater. We decided to test the truth of this fact. While purchasing more foam weather stripping for our drafty doors we became entranced by the store demo of a golden inferno promise. This electric heat dish sucked 1000 watts, which would blast many home solar systems, particularly without a handy fossil fuel generator.

That night we locked ourselves in our frigid bedroom where we taped plastic sheeting over the windows and mashed rolled up towels against the door. By the light of LED Christmas lights, we plugged in the heat dish. Immediately, the magical heater turned from side to side churning out blissful heat with an orange glow as we held out our frozen fingers. We sat on our bed mesmerized by the heat dish, like kids who had received the ultimate Christmas present. It seemed we had out witted cold, darkness and the ineffectual landlord although the inverter providing all this justice was straining under the pressure. Increasing buzzing

Utilities Nearby

sounds emanated from the inverter. A few minutes later our heat dish stalled and the last light flickered. There we sat defeated in the cold, pitch black. "See you in the morning" became our mantra.

Considering many people survived the dank gloomy freezing castles of medieval times long before electricity, we devised a new heating plan for our icy hamlet. We called it "The Breathing Tent." The theory of our "Breathing Tent" was similar to a canopy bed, although not as durable as the heavy pleated curtains that surrounded the chilly beds of tougher ancestral generations. Even the unsanitary folks who historically emptied their chamber pots into the street had antique bed warmers made of metal and heated upon the fire before bed. We had no gargantuan gothic fireplace waiting to embrace us with volcanic embers. Although our hippie straw house was lacking a hearth (as any historic home typically had) we prevailed.

We had paracord and a tennis ball. This apparatus was attached to the ceiling with the enveloping goodness of a cotton king sized sheet. Each night we climbed into bed certain that simply by exhaling we were heating the room. My relatives living in frigid London during WWII cozied up with hot water bottles and are the reason "Keep Calm and Carry On" is printed on throw pillows and dishtowels today. I could use a water bottle too, but raising hell tends to keep me warmer. Water bottles also chill down after an hour unlike Chihuahuas.

Medieval people living short brutal lives got by just fine on mattresses made of straw. With the comfort of our modern queen sized bed we were at least spared the act of beating a straw mattress to dislodge any bedbugs before hunkering down for the night. Plus, we had synthetic sleeping bags for extra heat. The goal in our breathing tent was to get through the night without needing to pee. Sometimes we woke up in the middle of the night and shined our headlamp on the temperature gauge we had hung from the ceiling in case we needed proof that we were suffering. We were still faring better than the Donner Party, but the Donner Party wasn't paying rent that winter in the Sierra Nevada cabin they happened upon.

One of my dad's favorite expressions is, "It's colder than a well digger's ass in Idaho." My family lived in Idaho when I was a toddler, but I never had the opportunity to ask a well digger if his ass was cold. In my little kid's mind I imagined a lumberjack digging an icy tunnel from an Idaho potato field to China. Now it was my ass sitting on a freezing toilet seat, living the off-grid low carbon footprint dream. I recalled an article about Alaskan outhouses and how it was easy to keep a toilet seat warm by storing it next to coats and boots in the mudroom. Just keep a toilet seat hanging on a wall hook and take it with you to the outhouse.

In a call to the apathetic landlord in Alabama, my husband alerted her that the winter temperatures we were experiencing were the inverse of her tropical heat wave. She suggested that we needed to run the out of code propane heater in the bathroom, prop open the door to the bedroom and as she put it, "Let that air circulate." The idea was to run propane heaters twenty-four seven and watch as our cheap rent house became the price of a luxury in town condo.

The only thing that circulated was our sarcasm and my cussing. I started singing Eric Clapton's Cocaine song replacing "cocaine" with "propane" because honestly in these parts, propane might actually be more profitable. The first week of December the ominous propane heater in the living room quit working. Someone had absentmindedly installed the faux logs upside down and a broken log chunk had fallen into the vent. Purportedly the ominous propane heater had been cleaned by said landlord once since installation a number of years ago.

Utilities Nearby

It was another cold week before the propane heater repairman arrived and showed us how, "Someone set this up all wrong. You know, these heaters aren't all that efficient. You might want to use your woodstove instead." The repairman's eyes darted around our hovel searching for the mythical woodstove that intelligent people have. "Man, tough luck." Even the propane man was talking about the benefits of heating with wood.

Off in the distance we could smell the warm woodsy fires wafting out of our neighbors' chimneys. Out for a winter's walk we ran into another friendly neighbor. By now the neighbor had noticed the high turn over of tenants. We lamented about how we didn't have a woodstove, both my husband and I feeling like idiots because we knew better than to have rented the house without a woodstove. The neighbor said, "Yeah our woodstove works great, keeps us toasty…Well, at least you've got a generator."
"Nope."
"Bummer."

Our landlord was too cheap to provide a generator and never mentioned having one would be a good idea. The powerful and whisper soft Honda generators cost a couple grand. Generators are one of the back up systems referred to in emerging solar books of the 1970's and this is still true today. Dark days of cloud cover do occur even in the sunny southwest. Short winter days are when nature lovers surrender to fossil fuels, even if they don't disclose this on their nature blogs.

We moved the bed into the living room, our next brilliant plan and then I came down with the flu. The holiday spirit was at a bitter low, but I was too tired to make a landlord voodoo doll. In my feverish and freezing haze, delirium took over as did fantasies of a new life somewhere else. Tucson's devil hot summers were starting to sound like the preferred extreme alternative to our predicament. After spending my toddler years in the Tetons I couldn't believe my mind. Snowy frolicking with the dogs had been one of my favorite past times. I wondered if the survivors of the Donner Party lost all interest in making snow angels too after their ordeal. The idea of Tucson burned brighter in my mind. I was spacing out like those people lost at sea when one of them decided they were going to the convenience store for cigarettes. The man slipped over the edge of the boat, purportedly into shark-infested waters, but the rest of the gang, too weak from dehydration could do nothing to prevent the inevitable. The remaining survivors were rescued shortly thereafter.

Living off the grid no longer felt like an exercise in mindfulness, it felt like being deprived and screwed over. Since we didn't have enough power to live a marginally normal life, we had to choose which things we could use energy for and which things would wait. In a decently built off-grid home such decisions were achievable, but we were living with the mistakes of the landlord's strawbale hovel.

Although I was not witness to man during the Paleolithic era, today's granola hippies claim that man enjoyed a bountiful life for millennia prior to the invention of electricity. This Schrödinger's cat is a circular debate because no solar salesman offered Paleolithic man such an option. We can only surmise that after slaying a saber tooth cat, that Paleolithic man and woman were content in their fire lit caves, sleeping on the hide of a wooly mammoth.

In our case, we would no longer use any of the lights in the house except two-dollar battery string LED lights we purchased on eBay. We would no longer use the small standard refrigerator because that was zapping our precious electricity supply. Outlet preference would be given to using my printer and charging my phone so I could listen to Pandora radio without plugging in a little stereo. Certainly there were many hours listening to nature too, but nothing goes better with off-grid living than Al Jarreau's Mornin'. I punched in a Zipcode for a remote outpost in Alaska hop-

Utilities Nearby

ing for more interesting and/or fewer Pandora advertisements. Virtually all of the ads were about how Alaska had a great 4G network (thus surpassing New Mexico) and how one political candidate was trying to finagle Alaskans out of gun ownership.

For the Alaskan off-gridder, a hunting rifle is probably more important than my lamenting about having no power for a refrigerator. In the frozen tundra, it would have been easy to build an underground food pantry. While remote yurt living on the tundra sounds quaint, eventually someone is going to pull out a gun instead of a debit card and go get dinner. This circle of life is a lot more graphic than ordering a pepperoni pizza. Admit that there are some folks that really are tough as nails and they are just fine living hours from a store in subzero temperatures. No, I'm not referencing the T.V. show, Alaskan Bush People who allegedly aren't really roughing it.

My husband and I obsessively checked our inverter and walked out to our solar panels. Sometimes we stared at them. How old was this array anyway? The manufacture's labels were weathered beyond recognition. We questioned the positioning of the house and walked around the property motioning with our hands, "This is where the house should have been sited." If the house actually had south facing windows we would be faring better. What the fuck were these people thinking when they built this place?" More importantly, "What the fuck were you/I/we thinking when we rented it?"

It was too cloudy to waste precious energy doing laundry in our off-grid washer, particularly since washing sheets would hardly stuff inside the tiny spinner. On an unusually bitter cold morning, we loaded up the dogs and three laundry baskets and headed toward town before one of my tires started making a thudding sound. At a soul less intersection between dirt and an isolated highway, we realized there was a nail in my tire.

As luck would have it, the morning was so bitterly cold that my wheel rim was frozen to the axel.

The consensus was to leave now and get roadside service later. By act of a non-denominational God, I was able to catch a faint cell phone signal and place a call.
It was Geico's Roberta, a real person in the town of Macon, Georgia. With a delightful southern drawl, she was ready to assist me in securing roadside assistance.

"Where is your car currently located?"

"New Mexico at a remote intersection."

"Is there a McDonald's or another landmark?"

"No, it's the middle of nowhere."

"You mean there's no fast food or a gas station around. No Applebees…PepBoys or somethin'?"

"No, there's actually nothing in this area."

"Hmm…Ok, what's going on with your car?"

"Well, my wheel rim is frozen to the axle right now."

"Wait…you say you're in New Mexico? Ain't it hot out there?"

"No, it's freezing right now. New Mexico isn't like Arizona, but I'm thinking of moving to Tucson."

"You know," say Roberta, "As a matter of fact, I've been thinking of being transferred to our Tucson office."

Immediately, I imagine abandoning everything I know to go work for Geico in the Tucson office. Somewhere beyond New Mexico was a normal life just waiting for me. This new life would mean I'd have peers that also worked in cubicles. I would be invited to weddings and happy hour while having a regular paycheck rather than hacking out life against the retirees of Santa Fe. I felt so connected to a living being who seemed to care about my plight that I actually wrote a positive review for an insurance company.

Utilities Nearby

The flu of December dragged on and I whined as much as possible. I felt like *Charlie and the Chocolate Factory* when the whole family (including Grandma and Grandpa) slept in one room hoping for that golden ticket. Sometimes that golden ticket was plugging in the humidifier for an hour while I dabbed Vick's Vapor Rub under my nose. I made a New Years Resolution that shamefully involved a thermostat. Lying in bed, I told my husband, "I might not make it out alive." That's when the pipes to the cast iron bathtub froze.

I suppose the behemoth tub was another freebie in perceived money saved when the landlord built her hovel. Water no longer came out of the faucet and the formerly licensed, but no longer licensed plumber was sent to the house in an untimely fashion. Like the man that repaired the propane heater who asked if we had a woodstove to use in the interim, the plumber asked if we had another bathroom to use and then offered his condolences, "Ah man, sorry for you guys." Said plumber was reluctant to proceed forward anyway based on the fact that last time this happened, the landlord was slow to pay.

Our plight was like that of the Donner Party, we would simply wait out the weather. On a sunnier day the exposed PVC pipes visibly meandering out of the house might thaw out. Now I'm not comparing my level of suffering with partaking in the consumption of human flesh. Historians also know that in spite of infamous cannibalism, not all the survivors resorted to eating the dead and they still made it to California.

Living in our strawbale hovel we wondered about the history this house. A little online detective work and we discovered that this home was the spoils of a divorce. Perhaps it was a waning marriage responsible for the shoddy construction. Damp straw walls probably were destined for demolishment anyway, rather than shoehorning in a pied-à-terre rental unit. The fortunate ex-spouse knew enough to walk away. He and his cat had bailed out for California. Clearly, he didn't care who got the piece of shit house and he probably got the better deal.

    We considered not paying rent to compensate for the weeks of winter endured without a heater. Instead we continued to pay rent on time and I took to vengefully peeing in the kitchen sink. Just a few months earlier I had been an upstanding citizen. Now I took joy in hoisting my bare ass over the kitchen sink and peeing. It felt like small justice against an apathetic landlord and a butt cold bathroom. How had I become such a trashy, disrespectful person in such a short amount of time? I considered leaving out this paragraph, but like the Donner Party, I want you to know what desperation felt like as morality froze over. Seriously, please refrain from writing to tell me what a scumbag I am. Let me just get these deep dark secrets off my chest.

    One of the things human kind loves most is advising others of actions that could have been taken in a crisis. It's a lot easier to discuss the road less traveled over a plate of chicken fried steak in the warm booth of an old school diner. It's another to make decisions while your reserves are low. This is why some folks have all the fitness in the world, but without the strong mental state to progress, some of us end up face down in an arroyo or delusional in the desert.

    Having lived lightly on the land not wasting any of our precious electricity on the small refrigerator or even a lamp, we decided to treat ourselves on New Years Eve. We wouldn't be BASE jumping into a swimming pool in Kuala Lumpur this year. Our outlandish celebration involved hot tea and using our DVD player to watch Disney's Pinocchio. The movie seemed much darker than my husband or I remembered. First Pinocchio has no street smarts, so he is abducted by a wolf. Pleasure Island was a freaky place.

    This sounds like a tangent, but I assure you that Pinocchio is the perfect film to gauge your energy consumption. It runs an hour and twenty-eight minutes, which is exactly

Utilities Nearby

how much power we had on New Year's eve. Before we had a moment to turn off (and unplug) the DVD player, we were sitting in the pitch black of our strawbale hovel. It was time to tell the landlord we were done.

Telepathy came full circle. A week later a letter arrived notifying us that our lease had been terminated. Basically we had thirty days to "get the fuck out." I guess that would have been more efficient wording rather than waxing on about how, "The tenant/landlord relationship just isn't working out and don't you dare steal the ten dollar non-cordless phone or the curtains from Big Lots." This was worse than a lovers' break up. We were way past namaste.

What did we ever actually love about this place? In the summer the rooms opening to the wilderness had looked inviting. It was a hike out your backdoor house. We had loved that it was affordable, dog friendly and out of town. Beyond that we found out there was nothing left to love except each other. Eventually it was too cold for sex. Was I really such a withering wimp to expect a bedroom to have minimal amenities, no different than National Geographic at Everest Base Camp? In my Craigslist post I made the joke about cappuccino machines. People either got my humor or assumed I was whoring myself out as an outdoors type and failing miserably. Never mind that our regular work came first. There wasn't a lot of extra time or energy to put money into someone else's house.

As my husband and I drove away for the last time the blue skies typical of New Mexico were once again, oddly gray. We had lived off the grid in the winter and ironically, we had lived within sight of power lines the entire time. We didn't get to actually use them, but off in the distance we could see the cables of electricity traveling to the horizon, by passing us, ready to supply other people's homes with the hum of power.

READERS' COMMENTS

Wow...I don't know whether to laugh at you.... get mad ...or be happy...but I settled on happy your article was so exaggerated that all the city slickers...And New Jersey yanks will go home or never come...off grid is so scary... No cappuccino or massage chair what...LOL...Jesus Christ what's your personal vendetta? You rented and lost your yogurt...You hate Madrid...You miss your big city apartment...what? I used propane for heat in every state I lived in Alaska to Florida, Chicago to Mexico. I'm not pissed like I said I hate whiny New Jersey yanks Cali trash...Go home sissy la-la's. Keep up the scare campaign its almost believable.

-Jim

Hoping to move to NM this year. Was getting real curious/suspicious about the off-grid, solar this and that, propane, descriptions and really appreciate your rant...ah, posting. I'd love to live in an adobe casita, but I am NOT getting on the roof to brush off the snow. I'm nervous about living in snow anyway. I'm thinking I'll maybe start with a nice boring apartment or condo.

-Margot

Thank you for writing this. Brings back memories, truly hilarious! I totally feel for your situation. I wish I could send you heat and light, (Currently in Michigan- 30 below and gray, radiator heat included however...) Although I was not planning on returning just for the "solitude" and the "great views", I may have forgotten many of your points looking at properties in the spring or summer.

Utilities Nearby

By reading your post, now I'm sure I won't choose the wrong property! Thank you again, hang in there, and may your lease end soon!

-Monte

Oh, how I miss the sun! Grew up in Colorado before moving to NM to apprentice metal smiths and study music. The green chili, (YUM) I have to order, which I do by the case! LOL; "Earthshippers!" Saw so many of those... online, some "look cool" and in theory, yes. In practice... wahhh wahhh.. Nope! Just too damn COLD! Especially because of the on the cheap hippies! I know I know; from Colorado, moved to NM to make jewelry, play drums, I have a ponytail, etc. Must be a hippie, right? NO! I went metal head!! I swear!! Haha...Never did have any modern heating while there. I was always fortunate enough to have wood stoves and kiva fire places though. Anyway, very fun to write with you Jes. I wish you all the best in ABQ and/or Tucson. Take care!

-Monte

Amazing and informative. Serious heartfelt thank you. I will consider this option no longer. Beautiful and heartfelt I can't wait for the sequel. Five thumbs up and ten stars!

-Anonymous

Subject: Off Grid Very well written post, absolutely marvelous. I hope you have a career as a writer, if not, you should seriously consider it.

Best,
Hamid

LOL! You are a great writer! You should do a blog and be read by more people than just a Craigslist warning. Seriously!

-Anonymous

I kind of love you. Thanks for a great and thoughtful post.
-Chanita

Hi there, Thanks so much for posting this. My partner and I were gonna rent an off grid in Cerrillos off of Goldmine Rd however, someone rented it before us and we were super bummed. However, after reading your post, I am so glad we didn't! Yes, it was incredibly beautiful, but the solar panels were out of date, the fridge was electric, and my partner and I both have online businesses that need ample electricity. The price for the rental was almost $900 and the landlord didn't mention a word about the winter upkeep. We were going to look for another off-grid, but have totally changed our minds after reading your post. People have no idea about off grid and I sure didn't until I read your post. So, this is a long winded email to say thank you!!

Kindly,
Heather

Wow! That is awesome work. Thanks so much for sharing. Very important to the future of creating the New Economy...that we get it somewhat right. Thanks again!!

-Anonymous

SUBJECT: Off-grid "insanity"; New Mexico style. I (for one) would like very much to thank you for the honesty and integrity of your posts. I have had friends get sucked into the "off-grid paradise" lifestyle by pretty pictures and

Utilities Nearby

stirring text on the advertisements, only to be screwed up one side and down another by the owners. Most of whom aren't hippies in any sense of the word, just financially over-extended idiots with non-existent moral structures.

Sadly, I tried warning them (my friends) off repeatedly by indicating that "primitive" and off-grid are two very different things. My warnings did not work. Unfortunately, especially for males, (not trying to be reverse-sexist here, just honest) they think they can "manage" any vicissitudes the situation throws at them. They can't, but they have to learn that themselves. This is not a test of manhood guys, it's the reality of renting a non-functional hovel from a con-artist.

Not to mention the fact that these landlords want outrageous amounts of money, similar to Santa Fe for the Carson, Mesa and Tres Piedras areas. Plus first and last. Often they want all of that up-front money and then indicate to you they don't want to sign a "rental agreement" because it is such a hassle. They are renting these properties illegally due to the primitive and unlivable conditions, and a rental contract proves that they know it. So yeah, no contracts.

Well, I bought some property in the Carson area (true Carson, not Mesa) about 6 years ago. I have a well-share, my dream is to get a thriving garden going up there and have everybody benefit from the produce. I have been incredibly successful growing: Amaranth, quinoa, sweet potatoes, regular potatoes, strawberries (in raised beds) kale, spinach, etc... in Northern NM and the Taos area.
Hope to see you guys up there someday soon.

-Anonymous

This post was utterly hilarious. Thanks for the sincere laughs. As a typical, poor, off-grid interested, Trump-fearing young-person who has fallen in love with northern New Mexico in the summertime, I also found this post extremely insightful, especially after becoming enamored with some of the "charming off-grid casita" posts listed on Craigslist. Thanks for the heads up!

-Tate

Thank you for taking the time to write this post. Off-grid living sounds great and I knew there would be some catches to it but I didn't know what it would be until I read your post. I was looking at how many watts to run household appliances and then I saw your post and found out all the problems that you talked about. The biggest surprise for me in your post was the propane cost and water problems. Anyway thanks for helping me consider the pros/cons!!

-Anonymous

LOVED YOUR POST! This post made my morning. I work in energy field for a big CA design firm where I think about energy all day long. Believe in renewables and all that, but reality is fossil fuels have given us quality of life and your post reminded me of that!! Loved it and the reality of "off-grid." Yes cheaper to camp too :)

-Lena

Although your post was very lengthy, I found it very interesting and educational. They do make those ads for "off-grid living" or "cute rustic and tranquil" homes sound soooo appealing. Even to someone who had lived in NM most of life. And especially appealing to the environmentalist aka semi-hippie/gypsy like myself. I know it's possible to actually have an eco-friendly home that actually does what it's supposed to but I'm guessing that's for the wealthy that

Utilities Nearby

can actually afford to pay people that know what they're doing to build it and make it work and plan on living in it themselves. So yeahh it makes sense that an overpriced one for rent is going to be some half-ass unfinished one that I'd be better off pitching a tent somewhere. So, thanks for opening my eyes. As a single parent looking for (an affordable and safe) place to live it's so very hard already to find. The "peace and tranquility and open spaces" sounds so great but the reality is not so appealing. The other thing that gets me is it's impossible to find a place that will let me have my dog which we have for companionship AND protection and so these "off grid" places will let me have my dog(s).. So I think "awesome" because these other so called "pet-friendly" places have breed restrictions. (I think I'll post a rant about that LOL). So the temptation of these "beautiful scenery" "rustic", "lots of land" "private" "solar" etc. sounds perfect... when you take off the rose colored glasses the true pile of Shit is revealed! Thanks for the insight! And as you can tell by my response.... I ramble on like you! But I loved your rant!

From, semi hippie/gypsy mama, (but not stupid) ;)

-A.

Hey Jes!
So glad I wrote you. Not surprised to hear folks across country are responding. When
you wrote your CL post, you stayed right on target. And didn't seem to have any other agenda than warning good folks NOT to do what you did! (Which is always accepted and acceptable, on practically any subject: Doctors, expensive schools, law school, jobs, dirty restaurants, property managers, car dealerships... Heck, I think they call it YELP.com). My weird romantic notions...like me...widen your subject a bit. I have lived and worked both professionally

and as freelancer in lots of great & big cities: NYC, L.A., Las Vegas, San Diego, New Orleans, Austin. You get the idea. BUT my dream was to always live in the country, country gentleman working from home, self sufficient garden, some energy panels (but not off-grid), UPS needs to get to house, friend to animals and insects. Garden for butterflies, bees and birds. Am I painting a picture? I even thought, of course folks live in the country to have their own ideas, to live their own lives....WAKE THE FUCK UP.

CALL! Attention, Attention (am I an idiot Or what?) It may be a Land of Enchantment, but the people are troubled. NM is practically in a race to the bottom, why, leading the nation in child abuse, animal abuse, and drunk driving. The only true NM garden is a junkyard garden! The good Indians- hmm, leasing lands to mineral land strippers, fracking, selling off water, not to mention those drab buildings marking the hwy – Indian Casinos, I believe. A plumber told me the teachers and workers at his school district race to the casinos with their Friday check of $250, and blow it all cause they are sure they can beat the house! For real!

Like you did, I am coming to realize…folks live in the country because they could never survive in a big city! I really don't even know if country folk would qualify for human - if human means to learn, to be curious, to pull yourself up cell by cell. To have a better line than "I had no idea" for everything you don't know.

Where will you go now? So, off grid living sucks. Actually, most folks intrinsically understand that, I think. I think there are lots of casitas and other situations for under $700 in Santa Fe…. Also Santa Fe economy is rising a bit. Home sales are up. Texans and Okies coming in by carloads to spend oil money. Have you thought of selling a painting of an off-grid "dream" home... to re-coup some of your loses?

On guard,

-M.

I so appreciate what you are doing. It is amazingly helpful and informative. Hope you do not mind my sending a shot of a place in Madrid I am looking at. It is described as "modern solar." It isn't the place where you were living with all the issues was it? It has a tiny fridge. Hope I can make this work through the winter.

Thank You,
Celeste

Thank you so much for getting back to me. It turns out that the place is in Cerrillos off Hwy 55 or Goldmine Rd. Do you think these infrared propane wall heaters are dangerous? There is one in each of the bedrooms and the living room has a small woodstove. Very good passive solar, but unsure what the structure is...maybe it's just wood frame and stucco. So insulation factor is unknown at this point. Cerrillos water that she says comes from a very deep well. The woman renting the place so far will only refer to herself as "C.M." Strange that she is not forth coming with her name. Only that she lives in the main house on the 20 acre property with her teenager. There is a $100 deposit for dogs $800 Damage Deposit Its about 480 square feet. Any feelings?

-Celeste

P.S. BTW I really want to re-read Dumas' book now that you bring up the Count.

I really appreciate you decoding the NM terminology. It does seem that there really is sort of a skeezy vibe around there while people try to sell you on stuff that isn't what it seems. You would have a much better way of saying it, I'm sure! Bwahahaha "propane" - that's a good one! I know what you mean. I owned a mountain house in California and I was so happy to see that it had propane wall heaters and a woodstove. After 2 weeks of propane bills, I went out and bought a cord of wood and never looked back! I lived in Sedona in a nice house in a nice place on a big lot and loved it but it was not rustic by any means. Take care and thanks so much for writing back. I really enjoy reading your stuff.

-Anonymous

I read every word. THANK YOU! Knowledge is power.

Grateful,
Casey

Thank you very much for this post! You saved us from making a huge mistake. We are new to this area and have nearly fallen prey to the sleight euphemistic taxonomy used in the off-grid rental advertisements.

-Anonymous

Thank you for putting this worthy email of education on Craigslist.

-Anonymous

GLAMPING

"There's no way those people are full-timers. People who live in the woods don't look like that."

-YouTube comment on a living in the wilderness video

After living off the grid my husband and I didn't take a camping trip for three years. I had always loved being in the wilderness and for years I'd longed for a rugged man camper to join me in the backcountry. I imagined wearing an overpriced high tech (i.e., polyester) shirt while sitting around a fire, petting my Labrador. I wondered if I would ever have the family that bought the superfluous camper ice cream ball. This must be the one gadget that no one in a survival situation would ever need. Yet people still rave about how much fun they had camping and making ice cream. I guess these are the things you can do after securing water and shelter.

My sheepish admonition to my mother-in-law on the off the grid horrors my husband and I had survived backfired. She asked, "Who's idea was it?" My mother-in-law has a good motto, "Quit whining and change what you don't like or I'll beat you about the head and shoulders." She grew up in the barrio and experienced a rustic childhood, which in hindsight was practically full-time camping. The eldest child in a Catholic family, her family home didn't have electricity or running water. Thus, you'll never find her sleeping in a tent, hiking in the backcountry or wearing a puffer coat. She regales the thermostat without guilt, blasting her furnace to just below a comfortable 80 degrees Fahrenheit. In retrospect, I am ashamed of my thermostat fantasies during that fateful off the grid winter. But like a lizard who's tail keeps regenerating after every brush with death, I return to the wilderness.

The RV demographic used to be retired snowbirds. Then "RV Lite" arrived, which is van living and typically a younger more diverse population. Those on the RV Lite track have a different philosophy than the folks driving castle-sized motorhomes. Class A luxury slide out living rooms are for people who never made a half-hearted attempt to fit all their worldly possessions on a single tarp. Arrive at the campground bringing your buoyant sectional sofa with cup holders. Such grandiose motorhomes require a special permit in New Mexico (at least the ones weighing over 26,000 lbs). In contrast, van lifers simply hit the road and have an easier time finding a place to park. These self-proclaimed "minimalists" are up to the challenge of fitting all their worldly possessions on a tarp. Spill over items make their way to deep storage in Mom and Dad's garage or a storage unit you're never coming back to claim.

Passing bloated Winnebagos on the freeway, especially those towing an SUV makes me cringe at the sheer excess of consumer America. Still some of the "simplicity first" vans sport plenty of luxury. Entry-level (i.e., beater) vans, typically rusted out Ford Econolines, have been sitting idle in a meadow just waiting for adventure. Mid range vans are operation ready. Add a kayak, roof storage, two decent mountain bikes and hope grandma remembers you in her will.

Utilities Nearby

On Instagram, @VanGirlsRule and I used to follow each other, but after a week I couldn't look at any more #Vanlife images. Just about every van lifer is still in the honeymoon phase. Anyone prancing around jubilantly in front of their van is clearly hamming it up for their next social media post and selling bras that say "Vegan." Why is it that none of the prancing and bikini morning stretch routines ever happen in the Walmart parking lot? These folks just took off last summer, the journey is new, the van is grime free and no one smells that bad yet. Other folks, such as Dave @Vanlifer, are a lot more real when it comes to authentic van living. Thanks to his YouTube Vanlife Bullshit Roasts, I've been a happier person.

I commend honesty. The jubilant van life crowd leaves out so much—things like emptying the port-a-potty or an undesirable night spent at a non-scenic truck stop. Such Instagram feeds are devoid of ever needing to repair something that isn't part of the "Pre-van journey" or "Outfitting the van." It's similar to the zeal of business start-up or a few months of hot dating. The annoying components are swept away for a pretty photograph featuring the adventure couple selfie.

I'll be damned if I ever comment my envy of the van lifer using excess emojis to express myself. "You guys are an inspiration" (thumbs up, happy face, cactus and the superfluous alien head). Sure, lounging around in beautiful places looking out the back of your van from your van bed is nice. Yet, no one discloses how many days it's actually been since they last chanced upon a shower with their gym membership in the middle of nowhere. I'm pretty sure the BLM slot canyon you just discovered doesn't have showers. Of course, there's always the truck stop showers, most of which are as decent as an average motel. It's one stop shower, gas and pick up a pack of Little Debbie oatmeal cookies on the way out. Tote along your fancy triple blade razor on the adventure of a lifetime while someone else (Mom) dutifully picks up your junk mail at your permanent address.

We've all been in positions where we embellish the greatness of something. How amazing it is to work from home or some dribble about how tiny living has created "more intimacy and freedom than we ever could have imagined." Even I've smiled and sounded confident talking about working for myself when in fact my ass is clenched at least half of the time. But it's all about squeezing the lungs out of life as opposed to living unfulfilled in quiet desperation like previous generations trapped in casserole land and old brown chairs.

"Living life to the fullest" is a hallmark motive of van life and off-grid philosophy, but with less risk and adrenaline than BASE jumping. Every time a BASE jumper dies, a fan posts a tribute video and the comments start flying like one of those squirrel wing suits:

"He lived by his own code, man."

Another chimes in, "Tax payers paid for the helicopter and the Search & Rescue team that hauled out the dude's body. Truly a selfish waste of S&R resources. What happens when someone has a real emergency?"

"National Parks aren't for those with a death wish."

"Well, he lived more in twenty-five years than you'll live in a lifetime".

"F you."

In the 1960's and 70's living in a van meant you were a hippie. Today it means you're simplifying. Free soul minimalists imagine all they really need is a van, a laptop, a phone and an internet connection. In reality you still have a bed, kitchen, living room, toilet, home office, dog bed and cat box, but now they all share the same eighty-four square feet plus a bastardized version of the word "loft." This implies that when you entertain and play scrabble during a blizzard that your game must be completed before someone

Utilities Nearby

can use the toilet that slides out from under the table that you also sleep on. Either that or your guest can go outside and shit in the blizzard. Particularly if you are partial to dispersed camping off remote logging roads.

In the egalitarian landscape of van life pooping, one can flip a coin to determine the merits of privacy. Private poopers will have to decide if they are more comfortable behind a shrub or kicking their partner out of the van in order to enjoy the portable toilet inside the van. Apparently, nature calling is one of the top questions regarding van life trepidations. The verdict always includes a five-gallon bucket, plastic bags and/or a spade along with the caveat, "only for emergencies." Whoever you are, my advice is to never travel anywhere without a few packets of Imodium.

Granted, small living spaces can be functional and comfortable. Doing away with foyers, punch bowls, china sets and useless living spaces is natural ingenuity. 2.1 kids no longer need their own room, which means no one needs a three-bedroom house. Everyone can get by with their own personal alcove. But who voluntarily really wants to live in a tiny house with two kids plus a dog and cat? No one talks about where they keep the cat box in a hundred square feet.

Pending pregnancy appears to be one of the leading explanations for why tiny house dreams fizzle. Maybe it's just an easy out for saying you no longer want to live full time in your Honda Element micro-camper. Now you've got diapers to dispose of and even if you're the up-cycle cloth diaper parent, you'll need a big contractor trash bag tied outside your tiny dwelling on wheels. The bag is destined for the trash or a chance encounter with a laundromat.

For couples that truly love each other, tiny living is a reasonable option. Anyone that can live a harmonious life whilst swimming tandem in the same tiny fish bowl possesses extraordinary compatibility. Tiny living is probably not the best option to save a relationship that is already on the rocks. I guess the equivalent of locking oneself in the bathroom during an argument would be jumping out of one's tiny house and run screaming into the forest. In love or not, I still want one of those cool 4x4 rooftop tents.

    I learned about the Golden Era of van life from my friend that actually lived in a van before Woodstock. It was an iconic VW bus and she and three other people bought into owning the van. True adventure meant no power door locks or windows and a manual transmission. Scruffy Sideburns drove the VW from Alaska to Guatemala. Once in Guatemala everyone went their separate ways when Scruffy Sideburns bought the van in full. Of course, back then there were no live social media updates of folks eating peanut butter sandwiches or camera footage of people sleeping in a van. Anyone who wanted to phone home had to find a phone booth and a quarter. More importantly, prior to smart phones you had to actually remember the phone number of someone who cares. That original VW bus is lurking out there somewhere and now it's a retro collectible.

    The contradiction in the ever-shifting definition of "hippie" is that the boomer hippies of the day were looking to avoid The Man (or being drafted). These original hippies sought a life free from societal obligations, opting instead for a life celebrating love and flowers. Now comes along a new era of back to nature hippies, all of them touting simplicity and fresh air while lurching forward to be product and brand endorsers for yoga pants. Even hippies are capitalists. Get out there and buy my "merch" because merchandise is so passé.

    "Merch" has to be the most annoying word of the decade since "selfie" made the dictionary in 2013. "Merch-pandlers" can't bail out after securing an ad revenue stream no matter how paltry, but someone will still make a full confessional video on why they are quitting van life. Usually, the person quitting has a huge late model Sprinter van complete with bamboo floors and a micro-sized woodstove.

Utilities Nearby

My first wave hippie friend who has now cracked seventy years of age will still sleep in a van during freezing conditions from New Mexico to Montana. When I brought her a cup of coffee one morning, her car doors were frozen shut. "Give me a minute to defrost the van," she said through the frosty window. She's the friend that adapts to anything without whining, hypoglycemia or strange dietary restrictions. When we drove into a snowstorm and my car slowly made a 360 degree spin off a slushy road into a snowdrift, she said, "If we're stuck we can just recline the seats and slip into our sleeping bags." On that trip she brought only flip-flops because we were driving south. When nothing phases a friend you know you've found the perfect company for travel and probably someone who really can swing life off the grid.

Van lifers are bestowed with more than incredible physiques. They also have perpetual reliable cell phone service even in the most spectacular natural locations of wind swept beaches, rock canyons and backcountry hut ski trips. When I wake up in the backcountry, especially in New Mexico there is naturally (pun intended) no cell service. Hard core winter camping or just a chilly morning at a designated campsite means your phone battery won't have much power for adventure selfies. Sure, a solar charger can bridge the gap between tech-wild, but aren't you forfeiting living in the moment? I wonder what the time lapse is between taking the photo dubbed "wake up in the wild" to actual WiFi connected coffee house.

Maybe I just avoid hipster coffee houses with WiFi, couches and banjo music. I actually like banjo music, but not to build a retro lifestyle brand or make a documentary on living simply or sell Subarus. Local coffee houses will love you, but not when you take eight hours to consume one cup of coffee and a strudel. Moving into the coffee house full time will never be an option. Sometimes people like to use diner booths as a micro-motel. This is why Frontier Restaurant in Albuquerque is no longer open 24 hours and closes from 1am-5am. Just remember to bring that pull over your head, nap anywhere pillow.

 Living full time off the grid, there's a good chance cell phone service may not exist. There is smugness from those claiming they shun technology, but sometimes phone calls are necessary. Like when you have to re-explain to the Santa Fe Parking Division that you did in fact write a check that cleared for the parking ticket issued to you five years ago. Remember this when you climb to the top of a hill and wave your phone into a specific juniper tree because this strategy got you a signal once before. Ironically, living in New Mexico there's still pockets of Interstate 25 between Santa Fe and Albuquerque where phone service consistently drops (Thanks T-Mobile, I'm still a no contract rebel!). The theoretical 3G or 4G "extended network" between the state capital and the state's largest city is part of what makes New Mexico a beloved backward state. To the surprise of those from San Francisco, New Mexico does not have ubiquitous 4G networks yet. Even if we're at the bottom in terms of economy, New Mexico will always be better than Mississippi.

 People use the erroneous euphemism "living fully" for activities like cuddling in their van next to their hot lover's dirty armpits. Their hot lover just spent two hours chopping wood. At dusk they boil water and take a selfie, shoulders shrugged, huddled around a tin cup of chamomile tea. The photo will be called, "Living the dream." They rise at dawn when there's still frost on the ground before the sun shines over the mountains. It's moments like these that get people to dabble in camping where the mind fluctuates on a spastic line between *Architectural Digest* or the guy that "gave it all up" to herd reindeer in the Arctic Circle.

* * *

Utilities Nearby

For our return to the wilderness, my husband and I secured the perfect campsite abutting a mountain stream. Primitive campsites are the ones without potable water, Astroturf rugs or satellite T.V. "No hookups" and the taped up water spigot would probably deter glampers until Labor Day. We brought our own water or boiled it from the stream. For two days our time was stunning and quiet. We had one solitary camping neighbor in the distance. The vacant campsite between us provided a wilderness buffer with the convenience of a picnic table and a fire pit. After a fellow camper nod hello, the solitary camper did normal things like fishing and sitting in a camp chair. In turn, we did normal things like roast corn and play with the dogs.

We strategically stayed until Labor Day weekend when the RV castles rolled in to try their hand at no hook ups camping. Some undeserving bastard would land our incredible campsite within seconds as we pulled away. It was our last day when a retired couple maneuvered a large beige living room with porch lights into the vacant slot between our blissful babbling brook and the solitary camper. Shortly thereafter the retired couple fired up their obnoxious generator. To drown out ear offending chain saw sounds the husband turned on George Strait's, *The Best Day of My Life*.

I'm a fan of many music varieties and will even attest to enjoying country music, but in the wilderness where my days are filled with eating sustainably caught sardines, baking potatoes on coals and keeping my spork clean, in the silence of the mountains, I do not want to hear music. Keep that shit confined to the KOA.

My husband and I made efforts to mitigate the monstrosity and noise pollution. We took our dogs hiking deeper into the backcountry. First we had to pass through the group camping area with pick up trucks, BBQ and Traffic's *Dear Mr. Fantasy* blaring from speakers, the quintessential anthem for wilderness seekers. The Kingsford charcoal was heating up as the tabs were pulled on Budweiser beers. Cigarettes lit up and men made small talk. For this group, high altitude paired with alcohol didn't cause dehydration. Speed walking beyond classic rock's sound waves, we were finally in the backcountry where the only people we passed were Sierra Club members trying out their new trekking poles.

Hours later when we returned to our magical campsite the country music was still playing next door. It wasn't terribly loud, more akin to the buzz of a fly incessantly circling ones face while swatting the air helplessly. It's no different than the unlucky dog left to bark outside and the owner is the only person who doesn't hear. When you have neighbors (and most people do unless you live on Ted Turner's ranch) it means dealing with the mole next door or upstairs. Finding a quiet place in this noisy world is what brings many people to sparsely populated New Mexico.

A lot of New Age white folks (and I'm white, but no longer New Age) in northern New Mexico live under the assumption of an all inclusive, yet reprimanding universal force called karma. The premise is that no one actually has to be accountable for any of their actions in *this* lifetime. Hitmen are out of work because nebulous karma will set the wheels of justice right—maybe not on this planet, but in the ether of the universe.

Karma believers are the ones who say, "You don't have to be affected by other peoples' actions unless you choose to be affected." I say those people must live in a monastery and even then, some monk or another is going to forget to replace the toilet paper roll in the community toilet. If it's a composting toilet, the normally mindful monk will forget to add a scoop of lime powder or sawdust. But in a monastery, there should be nothing else on your mind except wearing a robe, breathing and voluntarily getting out of bed at three in the morning to meditate.

Back at our campsite, the country music is louder than the babbling brook. My husband is the calm, practical type, knowing that quiet camper hours will soon arrive.

Utilities Nearby

"Let's cook dinner. Just ignore it and pull the corn cobs out of the cooler."

Crawling into the back of our car I tell my husband, "I'm going to say something to the old man." Digging into the cooler, I imagine the stunner quips I'm about to deliver to our oblivious RV neighbors, "Take that shit to the KOA!"

Tact has no place in the wilderness. This isn't about survival, but my right to peace in a $7.00 campsite that supports America's National Forests or whatever corporation now owns the forests. My husband walked over on my behalf and politely asked the retirees to please turn down the music. It turned out the retirees didn't have a vendetta. The old man honestly thought nearby campers would be at peace with his generator if we could listen to his country music instead.

The problem with generators is that I'm not the one benefiting from this chain saw blasting electricity provider. Had someone in their party needed a medical device that required power, I might have tolerated the noise out of a small compassionate corner of my soul. But to look out my tent and see generator neighbors using their porch lights made me want to throw a tiki torch on their glamper RV. Camper forums are filled with people venting their frustrations on juke box/generator camping verses silent retreat style camping.

Our evening continued in peace. The retired couple pulled their camp chairs around their fire. I was witness to the last generation enjoying a pension. The wife read her book and the man stared into the flames at dusk, just like us. The only difference was they had porch lights and we had a two-person tent. In spite of our extraordinary differences on the glamping scale, each camp settled in with the sounds of crackling fires and owls greeting the darkness. Nature was finally in balance.

That zen producing moment reminded me of transactions on eBay where before you click the, "I have a problem with a buyer/customer" eBay ingeniously suggests, "First try to work out the matter directly with your seller/customer." So you go back out onto the playground and the same kid keeps slapping you. Then you tell him, "I have a problem with being slapped, please stop." Telling people to be reasonable frequently backfires. Every once in a while there's a humble moment and you're reminded that humanity does have warmth.

    I hold no fantasies about adopting the van life. I'm still a part-time camper. The novelty of bathing in an icy mountain stream wears off rather quickly, so does taking a shit at the gym. I could roll around naked in the snow, but I won't. Why is this even considered a bathing alternative? Yes, I know the people who do polar bear swims call it refreshing and exhilarating. Yes, I know Americans take too many showers and waste too much water. Yes, it's true the French and Belgians get by on sponge baths. Yet post-camping, there's nothing like coming home to a private bathtub and hot water. In New Mexico, there is a precarious gray area between naturalist and eccentric. One of my Craigslist readers called it, "Taking one for the planet," but I was (in his eyes) apparently "too pussy" to do so.

THE SANTA FE LIFE CYCLE

*"Oh, I just moved to Santa Fe, you know it?
It's a wonderful retirement town."*

-A conversation overheard on an airplane
leaving California

Unless you are thousands of miles from the adobe epicenter of the universe, almost everyone has heard of Santa Fe. It's the oldest capital city in the United States and the place responsible for keeping Pendleton coats in style. *The New York Times* recently noted that after years of a fashion downward spiral, southwestern clothes are once again in vogue. However, this cyclical fashion news never stopped a Santa Fe tourist from forging ahead in leather fringe and concho belts.

Santa Fe is a tri-cultural land of artisans, but now has more retirees than ever before. Real-estate prices have soared over the past twenty years. Most of my friends here have been older than me. It's not something I noticed until I hung out with the one friend my age who left Santa Fe and moved to downtown Denver, Colorado. This was just a few years before the San Francisco exodus began migrating to Denver.

My friend in Denver wanted to show me that I could be like her; working at a PR firm, eating bad Tuesday Tacos and parallel parking in a trendy neighborhood. She wanted me to see how the Wholefoods shoppers of Denver were composed of our peers. It was almost uncomfortable for me to be shopping amongst other twenty-somethings willing to pay nine dollars for pre-sliced strawberries and pineapple chunks. I was accustomed to long gray ponytails, baby boomers getting acupuncture and Sikhs driving Lexus SUVs around the Santa Fe Wholefoods parking lot.

For a while I wondered if maybe I too could be a professional urban hipster. Maybe just for a few years while always dreaming about raising bison in New Mexico like Ted Turner. Although my friend was still scrambling despite Denver having big PR firms, such traditional paths had never paid off for me. Being reliable, motivated, relatively confident and congenial failed me every time!

I bought a black blazer for a land less enchanted anyway. A place where I would temporarily trade in my fleece vest for the opportunity to prove I was a professional with a job title in something like marketing, consulting, brand strategist or content creator. I could have grown up and actually left New Mexico. That's what many of us do with a college degree, but even that doesn't really matter anymore.

When I traveled to the other side of the world (to get a normal job I didn't get), people introduced me as, "This is Jes from Mexico." It was the first time in my life that Santa Fe no longer existed as an extension of my self. Travel far enough away from the USA and people assume you're from New York or California, or one of those middle American towns no one notices. People tried to get their bearings wondering if Santa Fe was close to Las Vegas, Nevada. Being from a stigmatized place is something to loathe and revel in at the same time. It's like New Yorkers who move to Brooklyn, but still claim to love Manhattan.

Utilities Nearby

I've always imagined what it would have been like to visit Santa Fe as a tourist. To say you're from Santa Fe, especially to a Texan while you're in Texas means you are lucky. But the one thing I've learned about traveling throughout New Mexico is to never ever say you are from Santa Fe while in another New Mexico town. Just don't do it.

Once my husband and I were waiting for a table at a local restaurant in Las Cruces, New Mexico. Las Cruces has all the merits of a college town without pretense on the edge of open desert. We struck up a conversation with another couple and I made the mistake of mentioning we were visiting from Santa Fe. The woman's eyes squinted at me with an alarming scowl, "Santa Fe? We use to live there too until we moved to Las Cruces. How can you afford it?"

Her scowl felt like acupuncture needles and I wanted to blurt out right then how much my life really sucked. How I'd never had a job with benefits. How I was wearing overpriced Patagonia underwear but they were seven years old and I could really make a dollar stretch.

I mentioned the outskirts of Santa Fe being less expensive and how, "If you look you can find a cheaper place." But I was lying through my teeth. I was completely full of shit. The only reason we had a crazy affordable place was that we got it through a friend and our place only had one window that opened. We also slept on a pull out couch because we didn't have a bedroom. It was like a New York apartment in a desirable location but one that would still never be that great. It was the sort of place you could brag about, but one that was too small to physically entertain even one extra person.

Rather than waxing on about the imaginary affordable property of Santa Fe, I talked up Las Cruces and the regional differences of our state's green and red chile. I mentioned how I'd already picked up the local real estate guides noting that we could have a swimming pool if we just moved to Las Cruces. How much I loved Las Cruces because it was authentic and real people lived there. How I loved the restaurants selling both burritos and donuts. How I could only get gorditas in southern New Mexico.

New Mexico is the fifth largest state but sometimes people from tightly webbed metropolitan areas assume we can just pop over to Arizona and pick up something. There are both cultural miles and driving miles between much of New Mexico. Santa Fe is the glamorous sister of the state, the one everyone wants to know or used to date. When you're done with Santa Fe you might be willing to date Taos or maybe you skied right over there in the first place because you're more down tempo anyway. There's a lot of other great down tempo towns in New Mexico with stunning scenery, tranquility and good food too like Las Vegas, Chama, and Silver City.

You might know about Roswell and the aliens that visited, but after you're done taking pictures of one of the alleged spacecraft crash sites, discussed conspiracies, outer space, the military, science fiction and the time aliens took you up their flying saucer, you'll go back to sharing photographs of New Mexico sunsets. Maybe you'll see the bats come out of the cave at Carlsbad Caverns or drink Gatorade in the sun at White Sands. Explore the Gila wilderness. Please at least go visit Wild Spirit Wolf Sanctuary in Ramah, New Mexico.

Take a drive though Los Alamos, New Mexico. Even better, explore the mountains on a road bike. For the science geeks there's the history of atomic bomb testing and the Manhattan project. This must be the safest town in America. It's the sort of place where women still wear robin's egg blue button up cardigans. Los Alamos is one of the most brainy, highly educated counties in the nation. Since most people are well paid, it's the kind of town where if you left a laptop computer sitting on the front seat of your car, it

Utilities Nearby

would probably still be there when you returned. There is a little weirdness with the various laboratory tech area signs juxtaposed near ancient Bandelier National Monument and the Tsankawi cliff dwellings. Most of the houses in Los Alamos and White Rock are just really banal looking, but maybe that's because they aren't adobe.

Even with all that sightseeing around the state your fetish with having an adobe home in Santa Fe returns. I have always wished that my family could have been the one whose wagon broke down in the mountains of New Mexico. Some of my relatives in the 1800's ended up in Jal, NM, miles from Santa Fe. Jal is practically Midland, Texas with fewer amenities and also no mountains. Apparently, things didn't go well for my relatives in Jal and they made yet another grave lifetime error returning to Texas instead of heading toward Santa Fe. I guess that's why in the tintype photo I have they look like sad sacks. Although most folks migrating around the west in the 19th century have that same forlorn look, pro-creating and pre-mature death mixed with bare bones survival. They really could have benefited from some Santa Fe acupuncture.

After our off the grid winter, my husband and I opted to take a hiatus from Santa Fe and headed south to Albuquerque. Around here the breakfast burritos are two dollars cheaper. After years of my life in Santa Fe, I could finally hear the Burqueño accent, which I'd never noticed before. The phrases, "yeah, I know, huh" and "not even" are distinctly Burqueño. Santa Fe never really had an accent because it's demographically a black sheep haven, magnetically attracting people from far away.

I made sure to write a letter to the editor about the pithy housing of Santa Fe and it was enthusiastically published by the Santa Fe Reporter. That letter made me feel like I got one last jab at the town I had loved so much. My young brain was formed in Santa Fe. I had now entered my thirties and no longer signed petitions to change the world. In the absolute hatred of Santa Fe's housing that fell upon me, I wrote cynical rants that brought me a modicum of solace. I posted on Craigslist often. My cathartic ramblings included:

Familiarize yourself fully with the Santa Fe and Taos area and mesas beyond before moving to New Mexico. There's more than Canyon Road and world class skiing. No one will tell you how quiet Santa Fe can be on Super Bowl Sunday in the dead of winter, even with good snowfall. Running a small shop downtown at this time of year can leave you feeling as if you're one of the last survivors of the zombie apocalypse. It's great for locals who don't miss the tourists, but bad for businesses. Winter is the complete opposite of Santa Fe's high summer season hosting Indian Market, Folk Art market and the Santa Fe Opera. Summer is when I believe some repeat tourists erroneously decide Santa Fe is the perfect place to call home.

During the low season, post Albuquerque Balloon Fiesta and aspen tree foliage, but before it snows is another bizarre time in Santa Fe. My husband and I received four free tickets to the Robert Cray concert at The Lensic. The Lensic is a small, but iconic stage theater of Santa Fe's adobe downtown. The tickets came last minute since a friend had come down with the flu. At the time we actually lived walking distance to the Santa Fe Plaza. We pondered who else we knew that would enjoy seeing Robert Cray. In any normal city these front row mezzanine tickets would have been grabbed in a heartbeat. I put a shout out on Facebook, but logging into Facebook is a world of two-dimensional apathy.

In the hours before the spectacular Robert Cray concert, we wandered around the Santa Fe Plaza assessing strangers to share our windfall of two extra tickets. We presumed it would take a few minutes to find a happy go lucky couple, but this was an egregious assumption. Walking onto the second level patio of what used to be the The Ore House, we approached a young couple on a date. "Nah," they said, "We're going to the movies." We amped up our sales pitch, "But this is Robert Cray, you can go to the movies anytime." Shaking our heads in disbelief, we migrated back to the street.

The boyfriend of a meandering window-shopping couple was leaving for the airport and politely declined, adding, "…but please take the rest of my cannabis stash." We asked a group of rare college students studying in Starbucks on San Francisco Street. Next we tried offering our two extra tickets to an older tourist couple as they walked across the Plaza wearing a sweater that no local would ever wear. The husband responded, "She's tired and I don't like blues music." Clearly, strolling Santa Fe wasn't making these people happier. A father and daughter doing a photography project for school were also on the Plaza that evening. I could see a quick fading gleam in the father's face. "I'd love to go but, she's got this homework project."

Finally, we wandered into the Eldorado Hotel where we found the first normal person in Santa Fe. She was waiting for a friend who had just arrived from out of state. She was thrilled to receive free tickets as was her friend and we all enjoyed a great dinner after Robert Cray's jams. It had taken us an hour in the center of Santa Fe to give away two amazing tickets. This is an example of living in the "City Different" and is not a detriment to Robert Cray singing in his sandals. We'd go see Robert Cray again before Pat Metheny any day.

Some folks assume that because they visited Santa Fe during the height of summer, that it would be a great place to start an art gallery. Not one that is hobby backed by inheritance but one that actually sustains and prospers. This concept seems innocuous enough since Santa Fe is allegedly the third largest art market in the United States after New

York and Los Angeles. Those with experience in selling art in Santa Fe know that behind the scenes you'd better shake a lot of monkey cages to sell art out of state whilst holding down an adobe footprint in the heart of Santa Fe. You cannot rely upon walk in traffic year around. Still there's a concentration of art galleries that out paces more urban areas, however quality in contemporary art is debatable.

The people from Dallas roll in with big plans to run a shop only to cash out two years later when they realize that half the year the streets of Santa Fe are eerily quiet. In the winter no one scrapes the ice on the north side of Canyon road because not that many people are puttering about. Not even the Texans on a ski vacation realize that for Santa Feans the first quarter means "hold your breath, spring is coming."

That's why *Cowboys & Indians* magazine gets it's Santa Fe kicks on in August just in time for Indian Market. This is the month the Santa Feans on a budget put in their advertisements. I suppose it's similar to the highs and lows of being a crusty fisherman out of season. Everyone is hoping for a good haul and we can all wait for the ice to melt because no one has a snow shovel.

I'm certain Santa Fe County only owns two snow plows. One is a parts plow for the one that actually drives around on the snow days. The New Yorkers always wonder why a few inches of snow is such a big deal in New Mexico. The reason is there's no salt budget for the couple of mornings with icy and snowy roads. The other reasoning is that no one in Santa Fe is all that motivated to get anywhere just as the night of the Robert Cray concert. Better to wait for the cloudy day to pass and let the sun do the shoveling.

Some come to Santa Fe to have second "careers" as artists or writers but let's remember that Stephen King wrote *Carrie* in a tiny laundry room during a dark winter in Maine. If you can't find inspiration in a cramped laundry room to pursue your craft, it's doubtful a stunning adobe studio will make a shit bit of difference. In fact, I'm typing this very manuscript under duress without a spectacular view out my window except for one juniper tree and a lone chicken.

Santa Fe used to close up at 10 PM, but now it's 7:30 even on Saturday night. In the old days Atomic Grill was open until 2 AM serving frito pies and pancakes on Water Street, but those days are long gone. It was an easy place to go with my friend where we wouldn't be faced with a slumped boozer guy using the pick up line, "You girls coming in for a cold one?"

Santa Fe isn't like New Orleans or Las Vegas with on going conventions. Sweeny Center got demolished for a more grand hacienda style "convention center," but I'm pretty sure no one ever really considered Santa Fe as the beacon of well attended conventions. There are few direct flights from hub airports, parking is tight and the hotel rooms are still expensive even during the low season. Public transportation is practically non-existent unless you're riding Sandia Shuttle to the Albuquerque Sunport at 6 AM. while listening to a cat in its carrier meow the entire way.

The City Different is best suited for more intimate gatherings. Conventions and conferences are not the point of Santa Fe and if you're that kind of action seeker you'll have to leave. It's actually a very small town where you'll run into the same half dozen people, four of whom you don't care for, one whom is a neutral acquaintance and one whom you actually like.

When you run into someone on a hiking trail and strike up a conversation, the breathless person with high altitude sickness is a dead giveaway that they haven't been around these parts too long. When you ask where she's from, she'll say, "In town" rather than admit she is actually from Ohio. No offense, Ohio does have good antiques, but otherwise a friend reports that Ohio is "Hell on earth."

Of course, everyone is a photographer who came to Santa Fe for the enchanted light. The locals on Canyon Road can get mad that now everyone wants to do the Farolito Walk on Christmas Eve. Don't even get into an argument about the differences between farolitos verses luminarias. As far as I know there are only farolitos in Santa Fe, accounting for both the brown lunch sack candle set up and the small bon fires along Canyon Road. Luminarias are something that happen in other cities and states. Basically anything north of Albuquerque are farolitos.

The one downtown Santa Fe event that freaks out some tourists is Zozobra. Occurring during Fiesta every year, even those lucky enough to live in the Land of Enchantment still manage to have annual "gloom" to burn. Everyone can't wait to stuff a note up Zozobra about whatever is ticking them off that year. After nursing a frito pie for four hours and people dancing in Marcy Park, the sun sets and towering Zozobra moans up in flames. A few minutes later it's all over and everyone goes home in a traffic jam. It's all worth it because this is one of the only times of year when locals hang out downtown, and the low riders cruise around. Only in recent years has the Kiwanis Club (or some other advisor) determined that Zozobra should now occur before Labor Day so the tourists can also attend. It upsets me in the same way Alfalfa's grocery store is no longer on Cordova Road and Bert's Burger Bowl is now a hipster taco hut.

The afternoon before Zozobra I recall watching a man wearing polo shorts and khaki shorts make a phone call on Lincoln Avenue. Whoever was on the other end of the cell phone was getting the Santa Fe news, "Some kind of burning man event is happening tonight." Another tourist found this pagan ritual highly disturbing. She explained to me, "The little children were dancing...and singing burn him, burn him." I'm unsure why this surprised her. For millennia, groups of people in all cultures of the world gather around

Utilities Nearby

fires at night to awaken primal behaviors and celebrate rituals. It reminded me of a Halloween party for homeschoolers where the mother's burned their bras. Surely, that was far more disturbing than wholesome Zozobra.

Crime makes people leave neighborhoods, unless proximity to the Santa Fe Plaza makes it a short-term rental for people from Oklahoma. Short-term rentals are one of the pit falls in securing a decent place to live in a tourist town. With clockwork rotation my husband and I watched our neighbors unload monogrammed luggage from across the United States. This wasn't really a problem except the tourists were the ones with off street parking. I can still bemoan my car being broken into and having my sleeping bag stolen. Sometimes what's worse than tourists is having a local drunk yelling, "I used to live here before you did!" That morning, I just wanted a plate of huevos rancheros.

The following property listings are an amalgam, formed by Santa Fe osmosis that are typical real estate of the surrounding area. This is probably why you're wondering about off the grid living:

Real Santa Fe living is this charming overpriced guest casita, perfect for artists (retirees who like raku pottery and once visited Santa Fe a long time ago). The authentic adobe home is just steps from tourists on the Plaza and comes with room to park a scooter. Plastered walls and updated, this casita comes furnished with a Pendleton blanket. $2500 a month.

Charming Casita Guesthouse, studio efficiency with landlord on premises. Ideal for one person with no friends, pets or family. A great place for someone who has cut all ties to their ex back in California. Comes partially furnished. Near Saint Victim's hospital. $1100.

This casita is conveniently five minutes to downtown Santa Fe. It's ideal for one person who has never sinned and hates animals. There's a drunk across the lane that yells profanity at women, but it's only once in a while. First and last required. Security deposit $1500. No pets.

Love modern living? This is your Santa Fe pied-a-terre southwest accented condo! Perfect for the art collector, there are lots of nichos to display your kachina collection. Saltillo tile floors with chic stainless appliances. It's moments to the plaza too! A steal at $1800 per month. No pets…maybe a cat is okay with additional pet deposit. Please Note: Because I'm a constipated chemically sensitive egocentric, I ask that no perfume products are used during your lease of the condo.

Perfect for wilderness lovers is this rustic but fully functional cabin near the village of Pecos. It's steps from hiking trails and is freezing in the winter. There is a "delightful" outhouse and it's best suited to the person who can shower at the gym in town! Because it's out of town and there's no running water it's $40 off! You pay propane and you'll need a lot of it! Minutes to Santa Fe (if you drive the last 10 miles of rough dirt road at 50 MPH) $900.

Eldorado Gem! Convenient living just minutes to chicken litigation (I'm going to harp on the chicken debacle for the rest of my life). A couple folks who moved here from out of state have nothing to do in their art studio so they like to write letters to the editor and spend Home Owners Association fees in creative ways. This passive solar home in Eldorado is on a greenbelt where lots of unsocialized people walk their dogs. $1800 a month.

Golfer's paradise! This Las Campanas Hacienda comes with a Platinum Elite Clubhouse membership, extra thick terry

Utilities Nearby

cloth monogrammed robe and preferred golf cart parking. Cocktails are on the house and spa treatment options abound. You'll enjoy the burrito glow wrap and heirloom 'Chimayo Chile Facial' (it burns a little, but is authentically Santa Fe). A view of the golf course is just the beginning. Offered at $4000 a month.

This cottage/mobile home is near Chimayo, which is practically Santa Fe. It's close to the casino and the famed Catholic church, Santuario de Chimayo. Because it's only half an hour to Santa Fe, it's $1200 a month (okay, it's closer to an hour from Santa Fe).

Apartment in back of four other windowless mud huts walking distance to Trader Joes where all the hipsters work. Job pre-requisite: you must have visited Bali or India at least once. Extra points if you went to a retreat center. This mid century home is near state offices where smoke breaks are part of the benefits package. You'll share a laundry facility with other tenants and you can hang up a line to dry your clothes like the rest of the world. You can't use dryer balls or mainstream detergents. I'm a bit of a control freak so I would like you to meet my other tenant before signing any kind of lease agreement. There is room to park up to two vehicles, but the other tenant is currently restoring a Chevy Impala in the other slot. He's actually my cousin's second nephew. Asking $1400 a month.

This Rancho Viejo home truly sparkles. It's like living in Rio Rancho, only it costs twice as much because this is Santa Fe. These cheaply built homes are conveniently located to Santa Fe's south side Super Walmart and anywhere America, only all structures are brown stucco. Soaring ceilings, southwest accents (i.e., a nicho) and new carpet. The unfinished one car garage is perfect for your Smart Car. These are just a few of the amenities.

Apartment off Airport Road. Cheaper than the up and coming Hickox Street area only there's no trendy hipster cafe near by. Shoot-em up style, double door locks with a discount. If this were any other barrio it would be a bargain. Small pet considered but I'm thinking no.

References required. No pets please because I'm a landlord and prefer pets go to the shelter rather than have a home. I love to deny renters the companionship of a pet. I'm also ignorant of cats and dogs or somehow just prefer cats. One cat. That's when I'm feeling cute, cuddly and semi-altruistic. But usually I hold on to decades old grudges against my family and got a huge trust find which enabled me to have this over priced rental property practically on the Santa Fe plaza. No pets.

 Bienvenidos to Santa Fe living! Yes, it was a bitter time in my life when I wrote the above. No, you can't have your red chile on the side and eat it too. Tourists who just discovered breakfast enchiladas at Tia Sophias, please eat it the way nature intended. Believe it or not, even after walking through downtown Santa Fe hotel lobbies and grumbling about tourists, I still enjoy listening to Ottmar Liebert's *Santa Fe*. It will always be the quintessential Santa Fe soundtrack and a few lucky people will always remember watching Ottmar Libert strumming his guitar at a wedding.
 Despite all that misanthropic thinking, somewhere in my Grinch heart I still care about people and northern New Mexico. Some of the best times of my life happened in Santa Fe: Burning my annual gloom at Zozobra, working downtown until I was downsized, finding the love of my life, hiking with great dogs, the chile relleno at Del Charro, playing marimbas with the other homeschooled kids, walking dogs at the old animal shelter. Would I really let a handful of miserable people and high rent deter me from making a Santa Fe come back? Never. Because in every

Utilities Nearby

western film the protagonist returns, maybe not until the sequel, but they'll be back, even if they died in the original! That's a common event for ex-Santa Feans. The love-haters and the angry-sex reunions with the town which they hate-love. The return happens bashing grocery carts on the frozen aisle or the low sodium boxed soups section. Sometimes it happens at the olive bar because even starving artists somehow can always afford stuffed olives.

It's a re-enactment of First Friday's art gallery walks where people dust cracker crumbs off their black sweater and look at conceptual mixed media. Typically people who loiter near the olive bar are looking for a date, but in the end they run into the old friend whom they once took exercise classes with at the Santa Fe Community College, "Hey, I thought you moved to Toronto?"

"Yeah, I'm back!"

It's usually anticlimactic and the conversation becomes olives stuffed with garlic or olives stuffed with blue cheese? Wistfully someone will segue out of the olives: "Well, after my cat gets acupuncture for a slipped disk, we should have coffee." You don't even have her number anymore, but I'm sure you can re-friend her on Facebook.

For those that stick around Santa Fe, you'll watch people move away only to bump into them again a year or two later. Occasionally it will be five or more years, but the clock always strikes twelve. The exception to this are folks that moved to Santa Fe under the pre-tense that it would be like Indian Market all year long. They experienced an infatuation with a place and after living in a pueblo style home with sunset views they decide to move "closer to the kids."

The kids live back east in a place with real jobs and even though it's polluted, it's still home. Santa Fe will be the failed love affair that is always remembered. Years later they will tell people how they once "lived in Santa Fe." Just remember that the one person who moved back to New Jersey regrets her decision.

READERS' COMMENTS

I just moved back to WA after 8 long years in NM! Never again!

-Kate

LOVE this!!! I got stuck here 42 years ago and am finally leaving this corrupt hell-hole filled with drunks & thieves. The only things I'll miss are the clouds, chile and the Indians :)

-Sandra

WOW, thanks for that! Sooner or later maybe these unprincipled landlords will get it. I for one am not going to just sit and watch while these greedy assholes destroy the place I love.

-Anonymous

I visited Santa Fe many years ago and thought about relocating there. When I looked around I got sticker shock. I live on the east coast and I am use to high rent for very little but OMG live in a teepee for $400 a month. No thank you. I would rather rent a room in the ghetto at least I have heat and electricity. Santa Fe is a no go for me. What do you think of eastern NM?

-Karin

Thanks for warning everyone about this. I dislike how Santa Fe isn't affordable now for working folks.
I commute on the Rail Runner and my husband works in Albuquerque. I hear that 60% of people who work in Santa Fe don't live there. It's really hard to have a good quality of life on a normal salary. I think the place in town might

Utilities Nearby

be ok, but the landlord might want us to pay more utilities the more of the "grid" electricity we use. We're currently in Albuquerque too. I do feel like Santa Fe has kicked us out, and we grew up there.

-Meghan

Hello, Thanks for posting on Craigslist! It was very humorous and really hit the nail on the head about renting in Santa Fe. We've recently been looking for places with all utilities included and came across a rental that has solar panels (that's how the owner said he can rent it with all utilities included). It's in town though so I'm not sure if the house is still on grid. The unit has 2 tiny wall electric heaters in each room and overall it was pretty cold. Something about the place raised a flag for me and I wanted your opinion. Is this one of those places to beware of?

https://santafe.craigslist.org/apa/...

-Anonymous

Thanks for your post! It's nice to see some honesty on here. My partner and I recently moved to the Santa Fe area and quickly became well aquatinted with the rental situation. Thankfully we avoided the off grid rentals. Keep posting!

-Anonymous

How sad. I left Santa Fe in 1983 and wouldn't live there again for the same reasons. And I'm an old-fart veterinarian with 2 dogs and 4 cats. Keep looking but it will never change. My sincere condolences....

P.S. - At least haggle for reduced rent in winter when you will be using the propane - that is only fair.
The rest of the warm months it is virtually nothing.

-Kim

Subject: CAUTION: OFF GRID HOMES INFORMATION

Hey Jes... is it you?

http://santafe.craigslist.org/apa/...

Happy Birthday!!! I O U a marg or two. I should be coming out in a week or so. Been collecting possible houses to check out. Has been a refresher course on the delightful absurdity that we call New Mexico. Fortunately, I'm living in a quagmire so any move (aside from earth berms with snakes) will be a horizontal move. Glad to recognize your voice and have a swell birthday. I'll let you know when I'm breezing through and you pick a place- I'm buying.

-Kim

Jes, Santa Fe is an adobe Austin. Whatever quirks and idiosyncratic lovelies have forever vanished; this was a large part of the reason I left Austin after 25 years. I'm not naïve enough to believe these special places will freeze in time, but I am amazed that new people move there, trot around and pee on these places to mark them and then incorporate "chic industrial" and middle eastern influence on the sublime culture that attracted them in the first place.

I live/work/communicate better with animals; my own species seems fairly messed up. Jaded? Yes and at 59 somewhat proud of that and a well-tended cynicism. I will wind up in

Utilities Nearby

north central NM hopefully by March. Fewer adobe Buddhas. Santa Fe will remain in my heart as an exotic landing place for a 23 year old hippie child many years ago. Memories sometimes beat reality.

I'm headed back out in a few weeks to check on adobe abodes and work. Will shoot through Santa Fe if you ever want to get a margarita- I prefer the cider margaritas at Rancho de Chimayo and admittedly had to look up what Silver Coin means. Meantime, good luck on your travels. Tackle only things you can either change or laugh at, don't sweat the rest.

-Kim

P.S. Found a great old adobe to rent in Dixon! Moving mid-March. Doesn't look like fodder for verbal abuse, but one never knows.

Nicely written. That is a well thought out post. We are moving to Santa Fe from California Aug 1st. If you know of anything under $1300, let me know.

Cheers, Kevin

Craigslist warning in NM. Thank you so much!!! We live in a 'burb in CA now and this is sooooo helpful. Keep these tips coming!!

:) –Anonymous

Just wanted to say thank you. You are appreciated. With rents OUT of control every bit of information is important for the renter.

-Newman

I just wanted to thank you for your very informative post. I am pretty sure that I was considering renting the house to which you were referring. Thank you. Thank you. Thank you.

-Tony

Today we saw your former landlord who accused you of "stealing." Somehow we do not think this is so. Even though there are two sides to every "story", we absolutely lean toward what you have said in your posts, as we have had some terrible experiences with landlords in the city of Santa Fe. We hope this all works out for you and that you can resolve your issues with the owner.
-Anonymous

I'm not surprised hearing your story about the off-grid house. "Off the grid" or "sustainable" sometimes seems like a way of saying "too cheap to pay for adequate finishes." I think going to live in ABQ will be a nice change for someone like you that has a progressive and honest approach to life. Sounds like you love the Land of Enchantment but have not fallen for the illusions. I have grown to like ABQ more and more since my girls have been living down there. There is a young vibrancy and lack of pretense that is the complete opposite of what you find in Santa Fe. I now understand why people in ABQ roll their eyes when I say I'm from Santa Fe! (Kind of embarrassing!) Anyway, I enjoyed reading your email and want you to know that I think you are a special person.

-Anonymous

I agree. I cannot find a rental property that will accept my one cat! But it is not just old white Texans doing it or causing it; it is everyone. People are coming to Santa Fe from all over and landowners are also from all over. I estimate only 20 – 25 percent of the rental housing accepts a small pet. My favorite ad on Craigslist was for an all concrete geometric dome with concrete floors but the owner would still not accept one cat.!?!

-LeaAnn

Well said!!! ABSOLUTELY AGREEING WITH YOU!!!!!!! And the ones who say they do "accept" pets charge an outrageous non-refundable pet deposit! Which is only because they want MORE money - not the pets. I looked at the very loose Craigslist by-laws. It seems it is against their "code" to say a property is for "ideal for one." Yet, it seems half of Santa Fe is full of "ideal for one". What lonely people. Devoid of both human contact or a pet. Currently living and renting one of the coldest "hand built" homes near Santa Fe.

-Anonymous

We totally empathize with you about the disgusting rental conditions in Santa Fe. Lived for about 5 months in a downtown Santa Fe location for $875/month PLUS utilities. There was no heat source in the bathroom, bedroom and kitchen. The roof leaked cold air and water. Cracks developed all along the ceilings and walls with obvious water leaks into the walls. Cracks developed in the tile walls in the bathroom (more cold air). There was NO venting for cooking in the kitchen. There were mice, roaches and ants.

We bought space heaters (3 of them) and asked the owners to pay for them (they said no). Electric bills - due to the space heaters - were almost $200.00 for 320 sq. We asked that the leaks be repaired - we asked for heat in the bathroom, bedroom and kitchen. Owners sent their son to the property - he fixed nothing but gave us his "explanation" as to how/why things were the way they were.

Called the Santa Fe City rental Inspector FIVE times - he never called us back. WE MOVED OUT! We refused to pay our rent for January - oh, and that finally got the owners attention, and now they are suing us. Well, they can sue all they want - we will fight them in court. We have documentation of this CRAPPY property.

These owners failed to tell us of TWO previous burglaries on the property. These owners failed to tell us about a CRACK house 3 houses away - they admitted they were well aware of this issue after we confronted them. These owners failed to tell us that the property next door was in foreclosure and that vagrants lived there with no electricity or water for two years. These owners failed to tell us that their two previous renters bailed on them for the same reasons.

DO NOT RENT AT ***...PLACE (3 units). Thanks for reading and I hope other renters, such as you, squeal loudly about what owners and landlords do here in Santa Fe.

Personally, we have contacted our state senator, Tom Udall. We have no idea where it will go, yet are hopeful. Senator Udall has been good to us in the past. Wishing you peace and serenity and that you find a great place to live.

The city inspector is separate from the county inspector in Santa Fe. The fact remains that 80% of landlord/owner renters in Santa Fe are dishonest, deceitful, and just want their money.
Best to you, and peace.

-Anonymous

Utilities Nearby

I think I've heard of that place. A friend of mind rented an off the grid place and it was a total nightmare. Glad you found a better situation in Albuquerque. I for one can't live down there. Right now I am in Galisteo, the place is over priced but the landlord is really cool in other ways. He said he was going to raise my rent and I told him if he did, I'd have to leave. He changed his mind and is not going to raise it now, at least for now. I want to move into Santa Fe but it is so expensive and you are right, there is very little for the average person. Santa Fe has driven all the youth out, the restaurants are terribly over priced, and nothing stays open past 10pm. I look around and all I see is the geriatric crowd pouring their money on everything. It makes me sick.

There are guards in the grocery stores and cops everywhere. This is what happens when the wealthy people come in from other places. It jacks up the real estate and makes a place unlivable for the majority. Santa Fe had it's heyday, now it is in a downward spiral of greed like many other places in this country. Best of luck to you and keep your posts coming about the experience you had. I am sure it saved someone else from going through what you went through.

-M.

Thanks very much for this info. You may just have saved my A** and countless other peoples A***s. Very considerate of you to take the time to share your experiences with your fellow man/woman.

-Anonymous

I really enjoyed your post. I have a job interview in the northern part of the state next week and have been looking at some renting options. I currently live in the southern part of the state and I totally agree with you about the inflated rental market in that area. Down in the South (Las Cruces area) a really nice house can be rented for what a one bedroom apartment costs in Santa Fe. This was a really good post and I am glad I read it and I am glad you took the time to post it. I actually thought about checking out some house with the "buzz" words that you spoke about: not anymore.
Thx

-Brian

I like to think of it as "Criminal Greed". I have rented for over 45 yrs and all over the US and never have seen landlords so greedy and local government not give a crap. Thank you for your post.

-Elaine

Thanks so much! This is so helpful I almost rented one of these places!

-Anonymous

Thank you very much kind human.
-Anonymous

RE: Rustic charming dirt floor downtown.
It's a joke. It's just a comment on the ridiculous expectations of landlords around here.

-Anonymous

Utilities Nearby

Well done. Thank you for educating all of us as we try on new clothes! Blessings,

-M.

Hello again, Thanks for the truths about the housing situation here in northern New Mexico, Craigslist is fun for a little while. My friends really seemed to enjoy my stories about life here and the way I describe how we made it up here for the last thirty plus years, as a full-time artist. I already made one nice children's book called, the story of the Santa Fe retablo man, fully illustrated by myself, fifteen color illustrations. I heard there's a device that the computer will write off a tape recording. I record, you edit it, and I give you ,like half, to produce it, I can also illustrate it. My children's book still needs a publisher, one of my thoughts is to teach the youngsters not to be caught up in system, that there are alternatives, so thank you for all the amusing reads. I'm a meta-physicist, I believe people's actions stick on their auras, from past lives too, that's what karma is, my wolf taught me to telepathically read human energy fields, that's why it's hard for me to live in the city. Thanks again. Godspeed,

-Mike

Dear Landlord,
http://santafe.craigslist.org/apa/...

It is illegal to list "one occupant only" as many Santa Fe listing do. Lots of old, lonely people in these parts. As a responsible pet owner, I'm disenchanted to see your breed restrictions and high pet fees. I would like you to consider more progressive pet policy as many people moving with their pets are responsible. An arbitrary breed restriction list is without reason (Dalmations?). Seriously. Furthermore, should you work to broaden your pet policy, you can count yourself as a contributor to fewer homeless pets. Your location looks nice and the price is certainly great, but with geriatric shelter dogs (one large) this is a shame. Punishing people with pets by charging outlandish pet fees is a non-progressive perspective of dog owners. It is old fashioned and out of date thinking.

Sincerely,
Jes

NINE SHADES OF BEIGE

"This gated community has sensible covenants."

-Santa Fe Real Estate Listing

After looking at Santa Fe real estate from abuelita's fixer upper in Tesuque to the house with a bathtub in the living room, my parents finally settled on a house in Eldorado. While my mother bemoaned the lack of closet space, "What kind of builder designs a house without closets?" the house was considered a good value. It needed some work like any house, but this passive solar abode with authentic brick floors could be a homebuyer's dream. Almost.

In the early days no one noticed that Eldorado had a Home Owners Association called the Eldorado Community Improvement Association (be sure to sign up for their e-mail blast). Since the 1970's when Eldorado went from big rancho to beige adobe development with sunset views, most people who lived there didn't really care what anyone else did. The HOA was something people paid into and for that they could hike the green spaces and use the pool in the summer. Each September everyone would gather at the community center to sell some over priced junk from their garage. It was live and let live.

Through the years of the 1970's and 80's (or after *Easy Rider* came out) more people moved to Eldorado and new homes were built and off shoot subdivisions were born. Eventually the original intention of building passive solar homes became lost in litigation about backyard chickens and solar panels. New homes were built with garages on the south side of the lot and the living room to the north, thus nullifying any passive solar gain. Although the lots average one and half acres, people could still see their neighbors across the expanses of golden grasses, cholla cacti and juniper trees. Sunsets, bike trails and green belts were no longer enough to keep people in a jovial mood. It was getting crowded.

The covenants were coming. Or perhaps for the first time, the covenants no one knew about were now being "interpreted" by the ECIA. People from New Jersey and Texas were driving around the neighborhood looking for happiness. Former authentic New Mexico washboard dirt roads got paved. Everyone decided the original neighborhood grocery store was too small. Someone said there needed to be a designated dog park. The only fights that broke out were between the people, not the dogs. Someone else proposed that there needed to be a special park for dogs under six pounds. It was determined that a few square feet of an arroyo would be fenced off for the little dogs to run and play.

Nine shades of beige were nipping at the heels of free thinkers and fleece vest wearers. Dog poop bag stations were installed. Signs were placed where no signs had existed before and for no particular reason. Like the sign that reads, "To the ECIA Parking Lot" which is placed just a few feet from the dirt parking lot trail head. One could surmise that the presence of dried muddy footprints would be enough to alert helplessly directionless souls that the salvation of the parking lot was merely steps away. In fact, through the juniper trees it was possible to vaguely make out the shape of a Subaru.

Because Eldorado is built on an expansive plateau and no one is allowed to fence or wall more than a few feet of their one plus acre lot, neighbors with binoculars have the ability to see what you might be doing that is in violation of the covenants. In many parts of the world there's nothing more secure than an eight-foot wall to shield one from the outside world. Adding broken glass bits and mortar to the top of your courtyard walls provides peace of mind. This is not allowed in Eldorado.

Freedom of speech is highly curtailed when living in a community with 'sensible' covenants. Political signs can be removed at an angry neighbors' discretion. The political sign policy means that if you don't like your neighbors' politics just walk over and rip the sign out of the ground. When there's an election, (particularly the small elections hardly anyone knows about) a few zesty campaign activists must reign in their desires to put out a sign until the designated time frame as defined by the HOA. If you're already wearing an "I Voted Today" sticker you should take down your sign. While you may legally be able to drive your car that still sports a John Kerry sticker, this is not allowed when making landscaping decisions.

There is apparently some wiggle room when it comes to certain covenant enforcement in the Eldorado area. This applies to the cheap neighbors that keep bus sized RV's parked on their driveways rather than pay the monthly fee for the "designated RV storage area". Although the driveways in Eldorado tend to be long and spacious, a few people want RV's to have beige covers that match the beige stucco of the houses. This strategy shields RV eyesores from the rest of the community but it is only theoretical in application. Even so, you can forget the idea that you can go park a tiny house at your friend's place in Eldorado. Don't even think about converting a vehicle to bio diesel at your own residence.

    Eldorado sounds like a place right out of wild west legends, but watch out or the Home Owner's Association will send you a letter. Your tipi and yard art may be in violation of the code. Someone who was never popular in school will tell you that you need to put a fence in front of your supplemental solar panels. But it will be a barrier fence, which is different than a real fence. Long articles in the community newsletter will compare those that like mowing down the natural landscape to others who prefer leaving the land untouched. It's like pod people in the Twilight Zone suggesting that we're all friends if you'll just voluntarily board the flying saucer. Even with your cooperation, the HOA will still want to read your mind and then they'll want to take your four hens.

    When you want to make an improvement to a thirty-eight year old passive solar home, you will have to present your case to the Improvement Association. There the Board member transplants from other states will spend copious amounts of time debating just what exactly defines a "structure." Is a shed a structure? Is a fence a structure? Should a proposed shed be allowed or should that homeowner get rid of some of their junk? Decisions like these are up to the Improvement Association. Even in the event that your home was grandfathered into Eldorado's new leadership, you will still need to ask for permission. Being "grandfathered" in does not mean you'll receive free slippers and a fruit cup. Someone will still visit your home to inspect your peg and string outline, determining if your intentions are in synch with the values of the community.

    Only nine shades of beige stucco are allowed in Eldorado (or nine that are perceptibly different from another). This means you can forget about the famed architect, Ricardo Legorreta's Enchilada Red stucco if you own a home in Eldorado. Technically there are more than nine shades

Utilities Nearby

of beige stucco allowed, however, I'd like to note that the shade "Sahara" appears indistinguishable from "Suede," "Pueblo" and "Egg Cream."

I also have some confusion about the perceptible color wheel differences between "Aztec Gold," "Bambi" and "Tumbleweed," In a world where "Celebrate Diversity" has been the quintessential Santa Fe bumper sticker, I can't quite wrap my head around the newly approved colors "Alamo" and "Abiquiu." "Alamo" looks suspiciously like "Café Au Lait" and "Abiquiu" appears to be pre-existing shade of "La Luz." Perhaps my computer monitor needs calibrating.

Now, some people will probably want to tell me about all the benefits of living in a covenant-controlled community and I suspect some of those folks will come from California. It's just an example. Two of my friends arrived in New Mexico from California. One of them still lives in, as she calls it, "Helldorado." The other used to live in a condo in southern California that didn't like her car. Something about the car being an eyesore due to a recent crack in the windshield. These former California girls no longer care or maybe never cared about having a Home Owner's Association.

Since I'm unbiased and for readers who are on the proverbial fence, let's take a moment to remember the good things about Eldorado: There's a lot of great hiking. It's quiet and clean. The night skies are devoid of light pollution. The air is fresh, there's a community pool. Most power lines are underground with a few exceptions depending on the lot. Every house can be sold with the attribute "Beautiful sunsets and open vistas." Crime is minimal except for that section in the community newsletter that supports "Anonymous tips" and "My-neighbors-are-outside-doing-something."

Most envy worthy is that Eldorado is "minutes from amenities and Santa Fe." Compared with many parts of the USA, Eldorado has a lot to offer the person who doesn't like chain link fences or neighbors with junkyards posing as sculptors. If you're the kind of person that doesn't want to fence in your acre or build a giant straw bale couch out front, you'll probably do fine in Eldorado.

Now that communities have Nextdoor.com, it's important to note your diminished anonymity. This website will also assist you in identifying neighbors who are trouble makers or those that simply have too much time on their hands. In another mesa top community, one neighbor's burning question was not about landscaping violations but, "Has anyone else noticed the silver oblong stationary object in the western sky?" To which another neighbors retorted, "It's probably a weather balloon." Neighbors such as these are typically harmless.

Never assume that living three hours from a grocery store will get you beyond the HOA orbit. A reader shared a remote property in question and wanted to know what I thought. It was a partially completed home on some acreage. The rock bottom price made the property more appealing, but with trepidation she asked me, "Is this an abandoned dream?" After reading the bylaws on the subdivision, I could see why the owner was selling the property.

There were unrealistic timelines for having a recreational vehicle on the premises while doing construction. In New Mexico nothing actually gets completed in one year. Livestock other than horses were banned from the community and anything that would not be in synch with the "natural beauty" of the area would also be in violation of the covenants. Of course, "Natural Beauty" is best interpreted by Neil Young and that could take a while. I'm pretty sure this included a ban on Enchilada Red Stucco. Don't' think for a second that just because your home is nestled in the trees that you can opt for green stucco paint. Green colored stucco causes neighborhood flair ups even though everyone touts the importance of "being green."

To buy land in a remote area and then abide by several

pages of vague yet stringent community by-laws is counter intuitive to me. Minimum square footage is the sort of thing that holds back tiny houses, but in a subdivision that is practically on Mars, is it really necessary to build a full sized home? Such requirements prevent people from living full-time in a camper on a small lot except in Tres Piedras, which has plenty of vacant lots and a squirrelly past. Finding a legal and decent place to park one's tiny house is a true challenge, although the growing pervasiveness is altering traditional rules. The next time you ponder a wilderness outcropping tugging at the heartstrings of "freedom" make sure you read the fine print.

HOA extremism can be a real disorder. It is theoretically the lesser of two evils; without an HOA someone might experience unpleasant visuals, noises or strange smells in the neighborhood. This could be a car on cinder blocks in a neighbor's front yard, the mobile home next to a hacienda, or the approved zoning for a crematorium that's near where you walk your dog. These are the everyday elements of authentic New Mexico real estate. Plenty of homes in northern New Mexico still live side by side in holy indifference.

LIVE IN A LIKE MINDED GATED COMMUNITY

In the words "Gated covenant controlled community," I hear maintenance fees I can't account for like the surcharges on hotels or airlines. Supposedly, this is to my benefit and includes trash removal at an exorbitant cost. Maintenance fees for condos cover expenses such as paying for a groundskeeper, but in New Mexico such a fee is suspicious. Unlike Arizona that casually enjoys backyard swimming pools and sprinklers, we're all about water conservation and desert xeriscaping. This means your condo will have gravel landscaping composed of pebbles in varying shades and sizes. Thus the necessity of a groundskeeper can be eliminated. In New Mexico, road construction zones sometimes have signs that read, "Your tax dollars at work."

No one knows for certain where these fees actually go, we just know the project hasn't been completed. This is the same as monthly community fees, which is one more reason to keep harping on your off the grid dream.

Apparently, there are people who have a burning desire to live in a covenant controlled community where (theoretically) there's no riffraff or unsightly neighbors. Real estate agents love writing home descriptions, "Live in a like minded community" and "Perfect for the golf or horse enthusiast." It's a place where you can donate a few bucks to a good cause, but without leaving your neighborhood or touching your face to humanity's buttocks.

People in gated communities often ameliorate unfounded paranoia with elaborate alarm systems. I'll always remember being the hyper-vigilant house sitter diligently pressing buttons as I prepared to exit one house. The alarm continued beeping and then an authoritative computer woman's voice echoed through the house, "Armed… away." It felt as if I should be ready to enter a war zone. My eyes darted around the living room. There really weren't that many objects in the house to protect. A few house plants, a couple ugly paintings, a hutch painted with that Santa Fe folksy rustic chic look, a cat box, an elderly diabetic cat. There was nothing of consequence to steal.

Living in an alarm secured home, especially as the house sitter acutely aware of the motion sensors, was unnerving to me. Even though the alarm system was disarmed during my presence, freakish red lights lit up in the far corners of the room when I walked by. Going to pee in the middle of the night, I wondered if I would receive a phone call any minute from the security dispatcher, "Ma'am is everything okay?"

Utilities Nearby

"Yeah, I'm just having a midnight pee in a gated community."

I guess such alarm systems are for people who don't want a dog or people that have a gregarious Shi Tzu that would go to bed with the burglar.

There is a vast chasm between the definition of "community" and a "gated community." In many ways, a gated community is an oxymoron. It excludes most people, while key padding in a select few driving a late model Lexus, whereas the idea of "community" can include anyone. As a visitor to the gated community you need to dial in with relevant information before the pearly gates mysteriously open. Before someone starts ranting about how I'm a socialist who dislikes safety and landscaping, let's all agree that everyone is a hypocrite at some point in their lives.

The retort is, "You don't want to live with 'those people' either." Which people? Gates or no gates, humanity will never be squeaky clean. Depressed people can still pull out of their three-car garage and take their cat to the vet just because they themselves feel lonely. They tell the vet, "I know my Blackie, something is wrong." After several hundred dollars worth of pointless blood work on an old cat they put Blackie back in her crate and drive back to their gated subdivision. All along the cat was fine.

People in nice neighborhoods still kill their spouses. Even a murderer can host a party and make their guests wear little disposable booties so the floors don't get scratched. Because who would suspect that a person in a nice neighborhood who liked clean floors would be capable of murder? Truthfully, most good stories are not found in a gated community unless it's a high profile murder or some other *Dateline* special. Surely your memoir is petty if you live in a gated community in the USA. I am interested in the life experiences of those digested through the bowels of non-gated humanity.

It's incongruent to me when a person lives in a gated community, yet spearheads some initiative on, "Giving back to the community." The existentialist could argue that all of us live behind a metaphorical gate. Perhaps I'm jaded, but it's not too different than a friend of mine hell bent on getting New Mexicans to appreciate New Mexico. You can't force feed people the wonders of the state they already live in just because you moved here and realized it's a cool state. She is a kind person who happens to be in the perpetual "Kokopelli phase." A lot of us already love New Mexico and we love our green chile even more. Sure some folks move to a place and we can introduce them at a podium as, "Aren't we lucky so-and-so moved here?" Usually these people write big checks to hobbled non-profits. I can only have grandiose visions of how my diatribe is benefiting New Mexico real estate.

Gentrification in recent years is now apparently synonymous with "white folks moving in" since living in the inner cities became trendy and suburbia became passé. Just a few years ago chain link fences and pit bulls were still in vogue. Those days are gone, replaced by the trendy live/work places with credit card rent-a-bicycle stations and local breweries. Areas lacking this trendsetter pace, for instance near the park dubbed by locals as "Needle Park," still scare clean cut people. These areas are sometimes referred to as "hoods." Such neighborhoods are an investment gamble when comparing the pros and cons to off-grid-mesa-bliss.

In real estate terms, hoods are called "culturally diverse neighborhoods," the fringe that just started gentrifying or might never. Keep telling the clean-cut, non-adaptable people it's a dangerous neighborhood in the hope of avoiding a Starbucks invasion and rising prices.

Albuquerque after all, re-branded what was informally, but collectively known for years as "The War Zone." Now it's the "International District" with street signage. As a kid I remember other kids telling me about the "danger-

Utilities Nearby

ous part" of town. In my young mind I imagined bullets ricocheting while sitting on a dilapidated adobe portal and swore I would never go there. Now I'm buying paletas (popsicles) and can't stand Trader Joe's and their Hawaiian shirted staff (just the one in Santa Fe).

The word ghetto has an interesting history laced with racial and religious bias. Eventually ghetto came to mean any neighborhood that was deemed crack house worthy, dangerous and dilapidated. Albuquerque, NM used to seem ghetto to me, but that was after all those formative years in Eldorado with the white folk astrologers. Some people still agree about burque's ghetto qualities and that is part of Albuquerque's charm. It's what separates Albuquerque from Santa Fe.

Albuquerque still has a culture that is distinctly local and truly diverse. I'll always remember the bus stop at Frontier, the restaurant across from UNM. The bus stop was removed when Albuquerque's Mayor Berry decided the city needed a trolley system from the porn shop and the grocery store in Four Hills to the porn shop and the grocery store on the Westside. My college instructor used to say that the Frontier restaurant was the "Crossroads of America." Stand there long enough and you'll see every walk of life.

I remember walking my dog around the UNM campus one evening. After the duck pond we were back on Central, famous Route 66, that iconic highway that Europeans love to cruise when they visit America. A woman shuffled slowly across the street in athletic shoes, walking on the folded heels. Her shirt read, "I Love Brooklyn." As I usurped her in the crosswalk, under her breath she murmured, "I hate white people."

I wondered if she was talking about me or just the average generic white person. I understood what she meant. Sometimes I dislike being white. In Santa Fe I could be mistaken as a privileged New Ager, the kind of people that have enough money to ponder astrology and acupuncture.

In Albuquerque, I could be mistaken as a white hipster, but one you never see in hipster places or micro-breweries. On Route 66 I could walk my dog and get a burrito without navigating that obsessive Santa Fe-introspection-of-the-self-vibe.

Whatever you are doing right now and if you do move to Santa Fe, please refrain from doing "spiritual work." Please. As Kurt Cobain said, "Come as you are." Well, he's no longer among us, so maybe that's not good advice. I spent a lot of my youth reading self-help books and trying to improve. So as someone who has been there, let me save you the time. Particularly, as self-help and spiritual work is a catastrophe that pointlessly spreads over the vegetable section of organic grocery stores. Don't smile serenely in that faux Santa Fe way either. Just put the bushels of kale in your basket and move on. Live in Santa Fe, but stop trying so damned hard. Be as screwed up as the place you came from and quit reading about self-improvement. Yes, you can still go get a massage, but please don't tell me the New Mexico landscape made you cry because it was so beautiful. If you feel a compulsion to play a wooden flute, practice before being within earshot of me.

I once made the mistake of asking a Native American woman where she had come from. It was an innocuous question, an icebreaker over coffee with another acquaintance. She explained, "It's strange when people ask that because are they talking about the land that was stolen from my people or the town I grew up in?"

I felt my pink skin of British descent flush with embarrassment. She had just moved back to New Mexico after a stint in a neighboring state and I was an insensitive white asshole. It reminded me, where did I belong when there was no place for me to go back to? There is no ancestral homeland waiting to embrace me. Hell, not one relative would take me in. The ones that would have are dead now.

Utilities Nearby

For the less adventurous folks, even New Mexico has a plethora of banal cookie cutter homes. It's a newer home with functionality and cheap parts that will break. Typically these homes are affordable. Overall it looks clean, livable and relatively safe. It's the kind of place where the real estate agents encourage sellers to keep the walls off white so buyers can imagine their own flavor of off white. As paint chips dictate, you'll discover more than a hundred shades of off white offering tepid individuality. These neighborhoods have cul-de-sacs and road names like "Paint Brush Court" and "Sunbaked Lane." It's anywhere America. Except, in New Mexico our banal cookie cutter tract homes are stucco, like Las Vegas, Nevada, Arizona and southern California.

When none of the above appeals, that's when you say, "I'm going off the grid" because you're a spiritual anarchist vegetarian who refuses to shop at the new Walmart. In fact, you voted against the Super Walmart. You're life up to this point has been uneventful or something you'd rather forget. For once you need to catch a break because you're too old now to start over. Off the grid is the last bastion of pioneer vibrations in this modern world.

THE KEN BURNS WEST EFFECT

"Truly where the antelope roam. Be one of the ten percent who can see the Milky Way!"

-Santa Fe County Property Listing

The documentary filmmaker Ken Burns often juxtaposed still photography featuring haggard pioneers with somber narratives read by Peter Coyote. A waning violin segued into the typical dialogue, "He wrote on his death bed..." Between live re-enactments, the infamous slow zoom created the illusion of motion now colloquially known by iMovie as, "The Ken Burns Effect." Many photographs since then have been parlayed into film utilizing this dramatic storytelling technique. It was actually invented when Ken Burns was still in diapers, long before the Macintosh computer.

A century and a half before the Ken Burns Effect, American colonists couldn't wait to migrate west. Manifest destiny enlivened the colonists who were tired of the stuffy eastern seaboard they had developed. The colonists presumed California would give them one more chance for a fresh start. This time they would take off their petticoats and go surfing after massacring the Chumash Indians of

Utilities Nearby

Santa Barbara and the legions of other foreign folks already there.

God, Racism and misunderstandings always managed to fit into west-bound wagons right next to Grandma's hope chest. But everyone had a chance to get in on the bottom level of the gold rush all because one prospector opened his mouth. The gold rush of 1849 proved far more compelling than the short lived run on Alpaca farming during my own lifetime. Smart people made money by selling shovels to the gold prospectors. After a few years of panning for gold, California was destroyed more by it's population than natural disasters like earthquakes, fires, mudslides and vanlifers.

Congested freeway systems, Silicon Valley, social media headquarters, Hollywood, the Pebble Beach Golf Course and chemicals known to the state of California to cause birth defects also put a damper on spirits. The Californians sold their crappy little houses, which were now worth more than gold. Some of the folks from San Francisco who were sick of high rent moved to Denver. A few others decided New Mexico might be a better alternative, including the folks from Denver because they didn't want to live with the ex-Californians or the expanse of spandex in Boulder.

It was Horace Greely's, "Go west, young man" who popularized the phrase by John Babson Lane Soule. After the Civil War, the second wave of western migration began with the construction of the railroad.

The promise of heading west had zealous settlers packing up wagons again and people were finally leaving Connecticut. Most of them were heading to California or Oregon, except for the Mormons who stopped in Utah and the mostly ignored state of Idaho. A couple grandma-estate-thieving cowboy types settled in Texas (one of which I am unfortunately related, lets call him "Uncle Stonewall").

After the battle of San Jacinto at the Alamo in 1839 the Texans started a pithy campaign called, "Life's too short not to live it as a Texan" (sorry, Texans, you got lumped in with DWI x 2 Uncle Stonewall).

While the Californians were coming up with a hundred ways Anglos could use an avocado, people in Texas were buying cookbooks with cornbread recipes and schlock t-shirts featuring Texas bluebonnets. When I was a kid I actually wore one of those stupid bluebonnet shirts and thought it was cool. Even though I never lived in Texas past the age of six months, I'm stuck with a glaring birth certificate proclaiming me a Texan.

Long before I arrived, The Santa Fe Trail, Route 66, The Big Texan's 72 oz steak, outlaw cowboys, trick ponies, rebel yells, Edward Curtis, Native Americans and a small herd of bison coagulated together and managed to float across the Atlantic. My Europe ensconced friends happen to live within close proximity of cascading American cowboy nostalgia. In Spain, my friend lives just a few miles from Texas Hollywood.

In Germany, another friend is once again living under the gloomy German sky wishing she could move back to New Mexico. Her home is not far from Pullman City, an amusement and theatrical park cultivated on the façade of the old American west, complete with stagecoaches and saloons in the heart of the Bavarian countryside. Here visitors can (apparently) enjoy Mexican food. I assume authentic German shnitzels are also available.

At Pullman City the romanticized American West lives on in wet t-shirt contests and classic American cars. Nothing evokes the old west like sitting around a campfire while listening to Lynyrd Skynyrd's Sweet Home Alabama and Freebird. American Southern classic rock is alive and well on the other side of the world right next to "freedom fries," otherwise always known in Europe as Pomme Frites. The Europeans may not have trashy Confederate flag camp chairs, but visitors can watch Native Americans and cowboys perform re-enactment shows of the by gone Buffalo

Cody days. In itself, Buffalo Cody capitalized on the first wave re-enactment of the old American West.

I once met the Native Americans who travel from New Mexico to Pullman City each summer ready to entertain tourists. In their suitcase they bring an exotic assortment of costumes. They meet a slew of people and keep the spirit of Native America alive in Germany. Maybe it's not exactly authentic but at least this way the Germans aren't playing the Indians and the money is decent. They have a great time and at the end of the season they look forward to returning home to New Mexico.

Like the many artisans that rolled into Taos a century ago, my European Union card-holding friend wants to keep living in New Mexico. She even brought her two cats across the Atlantic. Her knowledge of western history is extensive. She's appalled by how many Americans are largely unfamiliar with the characters that came before. In her foreign accent she assumes, "Everyone knows about the life of Buffalo Bill Cody, Tony Luhan, Kit Carson and of course Billy the Kid!" In her romanticized version of western history Mabel Dodge Luhan doesn't get syphilis. Mabel died in Taos, New Mexico and her house was sold to Dennis Hopper, which he paid for with the profits from Easy Rider. Even movie stars get hooked when filming in New Mexico.

I explained to my European friend how most Americans have only a tertiary comprehension of our nation's history. While we're wolfing down smothered burritos, building low riders and wondering about health care costs, contemplating history often falls by the wayside.

My friend was surprised when she learned that restaurant wait staff in the United States don't make a living wage like the time she sold perritos caliente (hot dogs) to customers in Spain. That's why we tip more in the United States and that's one more reason a lot of people don't have time to read up on history. Of course, average Americans will recognize the latest "Cody" making the country music charts while bastardizing the late legends of the outlaw genre. I will note that the name "Cody" remains a timeless classic of cowboy themed baby names.

Most people in New Mexico know that the city of Albuquerque is named for a Spanish Duke who never actually visited his namesake city. Burqueños still love to call Albuquerque the "Duke City." This makes me think of local meteorologists who rarely reference Albuquerque in the forecast. It's always, "Duke City this and Duke City that and here's our sky cam of the Big-I."

Somewhere along the way Albuquerque lost an extra letter "R." We'll never know why the namesake Duke never made the trip, but this was the 1700's and AirBnB didn't exist yet.

Either way the Duke of Albuquerque missed out on visiting Little Beaver Town. The western kitsch theme park stated up in the early 1960's but like a lot of start-up enterprises in New Mexico, the park failed. Perhaps the Lew Wallace curse of New Mexico was to blame. Little Beaver Town survived only three years before closing, even though it was just a few feet from famed Route 66. The ruins of Little Beaver Town remain a relic of kids playing cowboys and indians, paying homage to T.V. and radio heroes like *The Lone Ranger* and *Red Ryder*. Little Beaver Town was in fact named after Red Ryder's sidekick.

The real Red Ryder, Dave Saunders, was born in the 1930's and grew up in Albuquerque, New Mexico. The famed cowboy comic character, Red Ryder entertained kids for generations while becoming a licensed merchandise bonanza, most notably, the Daisy Red Ryder BB Gun. Most Americans remember bespectacled Ralphie in Jean Shepherd's 1983 cult classic, *A Christmas Story*, "You'll shoot your eye out kid."

The Lone Ranger kept do-gooder self-appointed lawmen roaming the west in search of justice. I refused to watch the 1952-53 seasons in which Clayton Moore sat out due to contract bickering with the studio. John Hart temporarily rolled in replacing Lone Ranger as if Moore never existed. I'm still a big fan of the original Lone Ranger but one caveat: He mysteriously owned a silver mine that financed his endeavors and produced his signature silver bullets. To put things in modern terms, Lone Ranger had a sizable trust fund. Instead of being a van life/digital nomad, he was just a well off nomad who rode a horse and wore a cool outfit.

No one could ever claim that the western was dead when the T.V. series *Gunsmoke* ran for twenty years. Sure *Gunsmoke* was made when people had few entertainment options, but even today, with bouts of the occasional hiatus, the western will always rise from the dead, just like zombies and vampires. When it happens, New Mexico is always at the forefront handing out free tumbleweeds to Hollywood. Our state doubles for other western states including Wyoming in the series *Longmire*.

My husband ruined my mild enjoyment of the film *Avatar* when he said, "It's just *Dances With Wolves* in Space." After thinking about Kevin Costner sitting in a tipi I realized my husband was right. I guess this is the dream many ethnologists have sought throughout world civilization—to be welcomed into another culture living in pristine natural beauty in the same way Barbara Hershey's character was in the film *Last of the Dogmen*.

Let's get this out of the way, you most likely won't to be adopted by a Native American tribe. This is a misnomer of divorcée imagination and coming to New Mexico does not increase your chances of settling down with an attractive native partner. This is quite the lofty goal when historically tourists simply wanted to meet "a real Indian," much less maintain dreams to marry one. I like to think we are beyond this type of blatant racism. There is nothing wrong with cultural intrigue, but people are still smearing Land'O Lakes butter on bread and driving around in cars called the Cherokee, the Comanche, the Thunderbird, the Pontiac and the Tahoe amongst others. While car models are widely recognized, many people remain confused about cultural differences between pueblo and plains tribes.

I won't deny the allure of falling for a foreign lover. This theme reigns supreme in romance novels, like the idea of escaping to another country or settling on a mesa. I only know this because Grandma read such bodice rippers of a good white girl, against her father's wishes, falling in love with a sexy Chippewa man. Naturally, I only read the teaser and sifted through a few steamy pages.

When the wonderful indie film *Smoke Signals* came out in 1998 I was a teenager eating lunch with my mother in Santa Fe. Adam Beach with his long black hair was also eating lunch and my mother couldn't stop looking. Nothing I said in that moment registered. I continued eating my enchiladas while my mother waited to pounce. When the actor got up to leave my mother also stood up to pay the bill in perfect synchronicity. Then in an awkward glow she smiled her compliment, "I loved your movie." To his credit, Adam Beach was very polite. I appreciated the film too, but I've never paid homage to the concept of celebrity. Sometimes people just want to eat a plate of enchiladas in peace without being recognized.

Not to digress too much, but Santa Fe's Folk Art Market also draws love starved women who flock every year to a certain jeweler man's booth. He does an excellent job of capitalizing on exotic sex appeal with seamless branding. Billboard sized portraits of the artist attract hoards of women who want to talk in detail about the new bangle they just bought. When they walk away, they can always look at the bangle and remember that moment when they almost married an exotic foreign man.

New Mexico's magic is a blend of cultures, largely Hispanic and Native. One of the most unique draws for visitors is learning about Pueblo Native American culture. As a kid, my family visited Acoma Pueblo. We bought beautiful pottery and I had the opportunity to walk down the ancient stone steps from the top of the mesa. This was originally the only route up and down from the city in the sky and it's one of my earliest childhood memories of living in New Mexico.

Over the years I've been invited to a couple feast days with different tribes. We shared posole, Hawaiian Punch and conversations. These were unique turn of the 20th century experiences, but I also recognize that I'm still a modern white woman that will never be a part of a culture that was historically decimated by my own ethnic background along with some conquistadors like Juan de Oñate and Francisco Vázquez de Coronado. Then again many cultures throughout history have decimated each other and continue to do so, including the clashes between Native tribes long before the Spanish and English, and everyone else arrived. Some came for conquest, others to paint pretty landscapes.

What is recognized as "The West" encompasses all that spectacular natural scenery that exists in the mind as raw and lawless wilderness. Basically, everyone east of the Mississippi was saying, "I need a place to be me." The West was the kind of place where you could kill someone and no one would notice; even if they did, there would be plenty of places to hide. Theoretically, out here you could walk away from the city and be re-born in oilcloth. But morality and statehood still managed to creep in bringing with it, wanted posters, laws and punishment.

Somewhere between John Wayne's 1956 *The Searchers* and Ralph Lauren's Rancho, the legend of the American West was brought to life in widescreen Technicolor. The red canyon lands and blue sky practically leapt into theatergoer's arms. Clint Eastwood's Spaghetti Westerns rode along side the late Edward Curtis revival. Ralph Lauren went hog wild decorating with faded American flags and Edward Curtis photographs of Native Americans. White people realized the ingenuity of the tipi.

For a while in the 1980's after John Travolta's *Urban Cowboy*, everyone said "The Western is dead…again," until the T.V. mini series, *Lonesome Dove*. Originally, author Larry McMurtry planned the script to be a feature length film for the icons of the American West including Henry Fonda, John Wayne and Jimmy Stewart. Hollywood passed because they wanted more youth driven films like *Easy Rider*, rather than stodgy old time westerns. The memorable tag line of Easy Rider continues to draw people to New Mexico: *A man went looking for America. And couldn't find it anywhere.*

Eventually, the screenwriter Bill Wittliff resurrected McMurty's *Lonesome Dove* into a prime time mini-series. Years later I would witness someone shaking Bill Wittliff's hand and say, "You wrote that? For real? That's the best damned thing I ever saw!"

Because *Lonesome Dove* marked the revival of westerns (and the end of the 1980's) CBS thought it would be a good idea to get around to the prequel nearly twenty years later.

In *Comanche Moon*, the prequel to *Lonesome Dove*, filmed in New Mexico, I would be unfortunate enough to be hired as a movie stand-in. Signing up meant standing around for fourteen hours in the 19th century western town of Bonanza Creek Ranch south of Santa Fe. The glass-half-full types could say it made for a journalistic Saturday. Lucky for me I didn't have to wear a hoop dress in the summer heat like the extras playing townsfolk. Instead I spent hours sitting in the shade of a golf cart watching Steve Zahn mess up his lines. Something about women, love and what life and death really meant. Who really cared about Woodrow's lack of commitment to Pearl? As sequels tend to do, CBS had a dog days of summer mini-series bomb.

Long after the moon had risen, the crew finally needed me. Someone provided instructions, "Put on this neutral flannel shirt and go stand under the lights." Twenty minutes later I was walking back to my car and would never be needed again. This was the film economy spearheaded by then Governor Bill Richardson that everyone in New Mexico was talking about. Six months earlier I had worked as a location scout photographer and six months later I would be given another chance. "Tamalewood" was here and people like me could stay in Santa Fe after all.

Well, a lot of my professional initiatives (dubbed "Make-it-in-New-Mexico-without-leaving-New-Mexico") actually have nothing directly to do with housing in New Mexico, but have everything to do with the folks that had connections on the west or east coast and then smitten with Santa Fe, decided they needed to buy an adobe home. Their professional lives were made elsewhere, not in New Mexico so their priorities were margaritas and going to cultural lectures, not lofting an ambitious young desert dweller into a career opportunity.

New Mexico's professional world has always existed off the grid or in those online job applications that go into the ether if they make it that far. It was times like this I wondered if I really was an idiot for spending my twenties in Santa Fe (minus that stint living in Africa where I tried to get a normal career in a city; stay tuned, that's my next book).

I was an impressionable teen when Ken Burns released the PBS mini-series *The West* in 1996. It was the most profound show since *Mr. Rogers* and *Reading Rainbow*. The voice of Peter Coyote showed me that I already lived in a desert paradise even though there had been a lot of bloodshed and ethnic sparring in the centuries before I was born.

At the time, I didn't know how many adults held fantasies of moving to New Mexico. Before I arrived, I said goodbye to my fifth grade friends who warned me about hantavirus being "all over New Mexico." I remember sitting on the swings at recess while my friend asked me if I was scared about moving to a place with a rampant deadly disease.

As a newbie kid in New Mexico, I managed to evade hantavirus, but in the months leading up to my family's move, I wondered if a mouse really would be my demise. Some years later, I would be living just a few miles from where a couple came down with the plague thanks to a wood rat. The black death of archaic history roamed freely in the wild New Mexico west. For a while, not even doctors in New York could figure out the diagnoses of the Santa Fe couple.

Life threatening risks aside, I bought kokopelli souvenirs and hung a dream catcher above my bed. I couldn't wait to visit the Rattlesnake Museum in Albuquerque. The words "bosque" and "arroyo" became so ingrained in me that they were vernacular English. Tumbleweeds were cool and Bugs Bunny was right about Albuquerque. Even the cartoons wanted to live in New Mexico.

Apparently, my generation is still consumed by western historical intrigue. It turns out I am neither a Generation X'er nor a Millennial. According to Wikipedia, I am in a smaller group of early 80's babies called, "The Oregon Trail Generation." This is because our most prominent childhood memories were playing early versions of the educational computer game, *The Oregon Trail*.

We supposedly learned all about the settlers pioneering their way through Native American lands, but most of us just remember that dysentery and cholera were the reasons we lost the game. We would sit in a computer lab with monitor screens bigger than today's microwaves concentrating on crude green line graphics with a dreaded slow melody alerting us that one of our wagon characters had just perished. Sometimes we experienced the prevailing pioneer family who made it to the fertile Pacific that would one day be developed into view lot live/work condominiums.

Utilities Nearby

Historically, communing with nature was an isolated experience. People read the quiet journals of a solo camper's snowy wilderness sojourn. Maybe we read John Muir or Aldo Leopold or joined The Sierra Club and imagined communing with song birds and foxes. What were once stories brought home are now live feed video of some guy shivering while boiling a fish head and commenting, "There's a lot of nutrition in there." In today's digital universe, a GoPro and YouTube has created a strange paradox: lonely survival is now "viral."

With glee I followed History Channel's *Alone* because I am an unenlightened person who has a tablet. Although I would quickly perish in the wilderness because I'm not a burly bearded man that can afford to lose sixty pounds, I see the attraction that draws so many viewers. People wonder what capabilities lay dormant in their DNA. It worked for Tom Hanks in *Castaway*.

While a few contestants on *Alone* failed to survive beyond day two, many people celebrated the win of Zachary Fowler's eighty-seven days in the wild. Back at home he and his wife were raising their two young children in a yurt off the grid while surviving Maine winters. Then right there on YouTube where people around the world explain their personal problems, Fowler openly talked about leaving the off grid yurt life for a large fixer up farm house complete with running water.

The decision made sense. People commended Fowler for putting his family first. A few YouTube comments went into a tangent about the water. Running water was just as contaminated as using chemical tablets in the backcountry. Running water wasn't important if the luxury amenities crowd could get beyond unnecessary convenience and be like the nature loving folks. Good parents provide or deny access to electricity. It's striking how one can make an equally decent argument for raising a child off grid vs. a child having a home with utilities.

It reminded me of when I took the writing proficiency section of the GED at the Santa Fe Community College. My essay topic was verbatim, *Which do you prefer: Country or City Living?*

While this experience was painfully remedial for a high school equivalency, I wrote with zeal waxing on about the things real estate agents like to talk about: "Starry skies and a place for my horses. Get away from it all because in the city everyone's an asshole, but out in the country, you only have to deal with one or two assholes, so in conclusion I prefer country living."

You might wonder why someone like me needed a GED. I was homeschooled and that coupled with too many years in Santa Fe resulted in being a free thinker. The university was unable to accept me if I couldn't handle writing an essay on country verses city living.

At the time getting a college degree was still considered an "investment" in one's future (except for those people who came of age in New Mexico and planned to keep living here). Apparently, I passed the GED with flying colors. What was never clarified was what type of country living I would be enjoying. There's a big difference between settling into a *Breaking Bad* RV in the desert (a la' Tres Piedras) and living out ones days on a western Dude Ranch featured in *Cowboys & Indians* magazine.

Cowboys never had swimming pools. Some of us are Billy Crystal *City Slickers* wannabes who want to paint in Georgia O'Keefe country, make tamales in Santa Fe and soak in the hot springs at Ojo Caliente. Maybe fulfill childhood western romantic notions of galloping on horseback through a mountain valley. Not everyone wants to spit dirt and dig fence posts so we parlay only the desired components of the perfect fantasy and forget the rest.

Bleary-eyed YouTube escapists comment on idyllic life in the wilderness videos. To paraphrase one, "I wish I could live like the Native Americans used to. I'm not trying to be culturally disrespectful, but just living, hunting and hanging out with my family would be so great." Even off-gridders with internet watch YouTube videos and then make comments: "This is exactly why I moved out of the city and now live 'for free' off the grid." Below that comment is a reply from a vicarious naturalist, "That is my dream too!"

If you are now living the dream, why are you still watching videos? We're you having second thoughts about moving into a remote uninsulated shed or did you want to commune with others in the digital world about why you left the digital world? In the end we all have to be with ourselves whether in an efficiency apartment, an RV, a house, a tipi on the mesa, off-grid hopeful shambles or the majestic Old Faithful Inn of Yellowstone National Park.

IN THE DEVELOPING WORLD

"Power outages will leave people in tens of thousands of homes waking up for a second day Tuesday, with no electricity to fire up the coffee pot or to take a hot shower."

-Unionleader.com

The acronym WTSHTF is popular amongst survivalist preppers. If you're the sort that dabs perfume on your neck you probably don't know that it stands for "when the shit hits the fan." Paranoid or just prepared, SHTF people like to have a plan. These people probably already own a generator and at least one disposable emergency blanket. They stockpile water and keep a bug-out-bag next to the front door. If you're ever lost in the woods, you'll want to be in the company of a SHTF prepper.

Another nor'easter was hitting Massachusetts. Chicago was bracing for the usual witch's titty ice winds coming off Lake Michigan and New Yorkers were bundling up in that cheerful "I-love-paying-thirteen-dollars-for-a-coffee-and-a-bagel-with-lox" kind of way. The power grid was down. How people would prepare coffee was almost as urgent as how people would keep warm. More importantly, how long would the power outage continue?

In the USA, both privileged (and under privileged) Americans actively seek a sustainable lifestyle. After taking a vow (and noble goal) of living without plastic, the more extreme version of "sustainability" typically has tinges of going off-grid in the modern world. Daydreams of tilling the land and lamps powered by the sun abut hairwashing with baking soda. Some people voluntarily walk away from electricity. This is far different than the communities around the globe that never had power grid access in the first place.

In parts of Africa, men risk their lives to illegally siphon electricity though their township. If they don't get electrocuted they sell the power to their township at a fraction of the utility company cost. Behind a popular shopping center in a large city, I witnessed first hand the cut utility cables running precariously across a road. The possibility of death pales in comparison to the convenience and ease that comes with electricity. These were people whose lives were off-grid, but that wanted desperately to live on the grid. One light really can make a difference.

That one light is also the biggest difference between people's expectations of what off-grid living really means. Having two hours of evening lamp time can be a new world of luxury or it can be the bare minimum in a Santa Fe rental. Being able to read a book late into the night because of electricity is a privilege as exemplified in a recent PBS program. For kids in remote corners of the world a little light is providing them with an opportunity to study before bed. With advents in solar technology, remote communities are now experiencing the true magic of having access to a very small amount of power. Even in places without grid-tied electricity, cell phones and solar chargers have forever changed the African continent.

Here in the US, people flock to sunny New Mexico off the grid properties described as "the perfect place for visionaries." While I've never been sure just exactly what off-grid visionaries actually do, this branding continues to seduce the back to nature escapist. Just how much electricity a "visionary" needs is debatable. Some people want to live off-grid because they are concerned about power grid attacks, which would leave all of us in a post-apocalyptic world except for the heartiest off-gridders. At such point, we would be unable to access Do-It-Yourself videos on how to turn a bicycle into a power source.

Overall the United States has a secure power grid compared with many other parts of the world. Other countries are the ones that have planned power outages in an effort to relieve grid strain. Having solar panels and a generator as a pre-emptive strike against paranoid grid outage seem over blown, but conspiracy theories and politics aren't the only reason Americans want to power their own homes.

Natural disaster prepping plays another integral role in being appropriately prepared for anything. As Mark Twain wrote, "I've had a lot of worries in my life, most of which never happened." Twain was mostly right, but sometimes hurricanes happen.

I'll always remember what Bill Maher said after Hurricane Katrina. To paraphrase, "Why didn't everyone in New Orleans pack up their Range Rover and go to their summer home?" Maher's dry humor was a point of economic class and the reality that a lot of people elsewhere didn't care about the people of New Orleans.

More than a decade after hurricane Katrina the French Quarter is in full swing and Mardi Gras continues, but much of New Orleans has been boarded up and forgotten about. My husband and I have friends there; one lives on the "right" side of Rampart Street. The other lives in the flood plain where housing is affordable (with a little mandatory flood insurance). In this part of town, if you had a bicycle and didn't mind a hundred percent humidity you *could* get to the store without a car.

Utilities Nearby

Here in New Mexico drunk drivers, drought and the bark beetle will be your claim to fame, but at least you'll never have to worry about hurricanes, mudslides, tornados or volcanic eruptions. One can only do so much in preparing for the worst and the worst may never happen.

For those who call flood plains, fault lines, volcanoes and tornado alley home, simply saying "I told you so" makes you an apathetic individual. History, economy, access to resources and greedy subdivision developers that failed to account for proper drainage, all make a contribution to the fall out of natural disasters.

Luckily for New Mexico, we manage to evade virtually all of the major natural disaster insurance claims, barring the brewing super volcano beneath Yellowstone National Park. In this scenario, even the SHTF preppers are going down.

Now that we've covered extreme paranoia in weather and politics, there's a questionable balance between self-reliance and community. New Mexico off-grid style is a paradox of outpost on Mars meets "I just realized I need peanut butter and celery from La Montanita Co-op." Just when you thought you'd be living under a rainbow of love some SHTF blogger tells you, "In the apocalypse, don't come to my house and expect me to provide for you." The gist is don't walk half a mile to the neighbor's house and expect to borrow a cup of sugar. You're looked down upon as the unprepared poor bastard who didn't plan like the conspiracy theorists.

Growing up in my house when no one bothered to fix dinner, I remember my Dad standing in the kitchen saying sarcastically, "It's every man for himself." That meant everyone makes their own quesadilla. Be careful what you wish for when you say, "I want to live off-grid and be self-sufficient."

In the apocalypse, self-sufficiency is a futile attempt to avoid the inevitable. Having grown up being able to satiate one's self with a box of cookies at the store, survival skills amongst the average American are non-existent. The question is whether one can survive long enough between catastrophic frenzy and adaptation to a new paradigm.

Your fossil fuel generator will eventually run out without the propane truck making delivery. Unless you are capable of manufacturing your own solar panels (and hoard tin cans), your solar panels and batteries will eventually need to be disposed of and replaced. Now you're back to humanity re-discovering fire while you live on a New Mexico property dubbed "Recession Proof House." Unless you really do grow all your own food year around or have some useful swag to trade out, the recession proof house is a misnomer.

Post-apocolypse, for the first couple months and maybe even a year, you and the lucky souls you invite will experience a gluttonous cornucopia of homegrown food and solar power. But then what? Your utopian society on the mesa will require a dedicated survival team and there won't be any room for social loafers or an infirm, but well loved grandma. This is no place for tube tops, tiki torches, s'mores and summer campers.

You will have to choose not who you like the most, but who possesses the survival skills to function under truly self-sufficient conditions. Everyone will have to pitch in and that means putting Grandma out to pasture unless she can shuck corn or contribute. Now I'm not condoning that in natural disasters it's okay to abandon infirm folks, but the case for self-sufficiency is not one of morality. It's about who survives and who doesn't. That means saving your dogs first followed by the friends and family who are the least hassle.

This is akin to living in the wild animal kingdom. Remember the *Planet Earth* series where the baby Zebra has to make a choice? Stay with dead mom or travel onward with the herd. After a few heart wrenching minutes, the baby zebra marches forward with the rest of the herd.

Utilities Nearby

Fans of *The Walking Dead's* early years understand what I'm talking about. Sometimes you have to leave the zombie infected person under a tree and keep driving the minivan until it runs out of gas.

There are the guys that spend Alaskan summer time naked and they get featured on National Geographic. For some reason no one tires of watching a scruffy mountain man wading into a glacial lake for his first bath of the year.

Videos of bearded men living in the woods have all sorts of useful life skill tips, but they'll still never gain the fan base of boobs, bikinis and cats. Of course, the water is cold. Sitting next to your apartment furnace you start thinking to yourself, "I could do that." You can, but do you want to do that every spring for the rest of your life?

Around the world people still bathe like glacier mountain man, only it's more typically the Ganges River and there's a crowd of others doing the same thing. You won't get that "It's just me and the mountain feeling" on the Ganges. Instead you will be reminded of humanity and the very real daily struggle of survival, but this time you won't be able to go back to that crappy overpriced apartment in Jersey City or Los Angeles.

* * *

One of my pet peeves is when self-described "former corporate executives" (never from New Mexico) suddenly turn to "a simpler life." These folks do things like buy an RV or "walk away from a high paying job." Personally, here in New Mexico, I've never *once* been given the opportunity to "walk away from a high paying corporate job." This is largely irrelevant to my generation because we never had that and it's not because we didn't spend all of our twenties dancing our asses off to move up the food chain from work-for-free-intern.

Former corporate executives are typically the kind of people who choose life coaching as a second career, only everything they did to succeed in life happened prior to the digital revolution. Some of these people went to Yale and they like to tell you about how they went to Yale but now they want to live in New Mexico.

It's the same absurdity as Annie Leibovitz teaching photography today because none of the old rules apply anymore. Multi-level marketing is now called content creation and influencing. It just doesn't come with health insurance and a Casio watch like it used to.

All of these facets of life assemble into the mindsets of those going off-grid and the millennial desire to experience life (i.e., settle for being a brand ambassador) rather than be a consumer like the baby boomer generation. It's one more reason that sales are down on sectional sofas, heirloom furniture and Native American pottery. People don't have walls anymore and when they do, they might be moving soon so better to settle for a Craigslist curb alert.

There's a misconception in the first world that rejecting the convenience of utility company electricity is cause for saving the planet. In my humble opinion, this action is not grounds to roll out a red carpet.

Unless you are foregoing electricity all together (and thus joining the millions of other people who have never had electricity) you are simply shifting your environmental footprint. Making your own electricity and more importantly, storing electricity requires batteries, which eventually will need to be disposed of or recycled. Both of these processes require energy. Let's not even get started on carbon footprints.

First consider that having the option to choose between having utilities or not is a privilege. For the most remote corners of the globe, electricity and potable water comes after the delivery of Coca Cola. Advances in solar technology are becoming a game changer for far-flung outposts (and

UTILITIES NEARBY

New Mexico too). Whether living in a rondoval in Africa or a yurt in New Mexico, we can charge our phones on portable solar chargers as long as the sun shines. We can charge laptops too, but as soon as you need hot water or heat, watch out—that's going to cost fuel no matter what you do. Climate controlled environments are a grand luxury.

On the grid or not, every person makes an impact by using resources. There's the slew of satellite dishes affixed to apartment balconies, positioned mere inches from one another. To people who sponge bathe in the woods this is an outrage. Almost worse than the gas it takes the UPS truck to bounce down your washboard dirt road to deliver the vitamins you never needed until you moved to a mesa in northern New Mexico.

Some of us are more energy hogs than others and some of us are finding ways to reduce what we deem necessary. As much as I vacillate between humanitarian and misanthropic Aquarian, we all need each other to survive. I'm a realist in accepting that my living-breathing-smart-phone-using-shitting-body is making an impact to this planet. How positive or negative this impact is felt, is open to interpretation and scientific measurement. Being a pompous do-gooder who sees himself as a separate self-sufficient being is simply a delusion of over exposure to the "Taos Hum."

ENCHANTED ABANDONMENT, DISENCHANTED SUBURBIA

"Diamond in the rough! Bring your imagination & a little TLC."
-Taos County Real Estate Listing

"Water falls from the sky."
–Michael Reynolds, Creator of Earthships

"My loss is your gain" is a classic sales pitch applying to everything from used electronics to real estate along with the phrase "plenty of life left." In a personals ad, you would shy away from such a description, but it's perfect for your old junk or used solar panels. Advertising irks me with the imaginary urgency tactic, "Hurry, this home won't last!" When a real estate agent writes, "Too many amenities to mention!" it means she couldn't think of anything to beef up buyer interest or she's just pitiful when it comes to copywriting.

"If you've been looking at buying someone else's failed dream, this is it!" Shameless piranha ambition is what took Alec Baldwin's character to the top with, "Coffee is for closers." I remember looking at real estate listings in my early teens, but back then I didn't know about the "Glengarry GlenRoss leads."

When I was a teenager, I saw a dream in a New Mexico real estate guide: 3000 square foot mostly completed cedar geodesic dome home awaiting completion. The listing waxed on about how the home was loaded with amenities even though it wasn't yet completed. The home had a green house, walk in closets, a giant sink to wash dogs in the laundry room, a huge fireplace and plenty of room for a pool table. So what if the electrical wasn't exactly in place yet? It was "mostly" completed. Know from this point forward that any plot of land with a slab foundation can be described as "mostly" completed or "in place," at least according to New Mexico jargon.

Like an online dating profile, real estate agents love to use the word "potential" to describe amenities that are theoretical. Maybe you aren't currently going to the gym, but you could if you met the right partner. Home descriptions such as "room for a pool, pony, guest house or four car garage" fall into theoretical amenities. "The property includes plans for a hacienda," is another example—perhaps a hacienda that rivals the style featured in the 1956 film *Giant* starring James Dean.

When someone abandons plans any sane person wonders why. Was it because they were tired of drawing diagrams to appease the historical association? Or was it recently discovered that the neighbor is uncomfortably weird, wears a coat in the summer and sometimes stares in your windows? It's not technically harassment, but you're not really sure. Was it that the property really doesn't have water and never will so you're reselling it on Craigslist, "Beautiful raw land, live the dream." Maybe the reason for selling is something vague cloaked in the all encompassing save face, "I don't have time to complete the project."

Many grandiose home terms are shoe horned into New

Mexico real estate listings. Access via a step ladder does not constitute equating the area upstairs with having a "loft."

The gated community with only three residences sans HOA sure sounded like a steal. That's when I looked up the property lines with undisclosed easements because two lots didn't actually have access without crossing the neighbor's property. These historic horse and buggy lots didn't foresee parking for a Toyota Prius or angry neighbors on driveway easement power trips.

Sometimes property listings in Santa Fe County read like a children's bedtime story. I sift through wistful non-coherent poetry about the Wells Fargo Stagecoach, the Santa Fe Trail and wagons west without learning if the property has utilities or if it is fenced. "Legend has it…" only goes so far. Water is rarely mentioned. Instead I'm supposed to be so transfixed by sunsets and turquoise that there are no further questions as the real estate agent sweeps me off my feet. Occasionally, there's the notorious bait and switch, "This lot is already sold, but we have others just like it!" "Electric pole on property" sounds like hidden development costs to me. You'd think real estate agents would be better off saving time and at least come clean with some basic bullet points before scheduling a weekend open house.

There are conclusions that you would probably surmise on your own without a real estate agent. For example, "You could live in the existing cabin while building your dream home." Real estate charm can sometimes make it challenging to discern theoretical amenities from existing backbreaking labor. It's like saying, "One could add a waterslide from a second floor deck that doesn't yet exist." Barring a HOA violation (and sufficient water rights) almost any house could have a water slide. However, I suspect this would instigate a scandalous article featured on the front page of *The New Mexican:* "Homeowner Installs Water Slide, Wastes Water." Santa Feans love writing scathing letters to the editor (me included).

Utilities Nearby

What exactly does "my loss is your gain" really mean? It's with deep regret that the seller is letting go of their partially completed home due to a sick mother-in-law in another state. More likely, it's that the seller is desperate to be free of the house like a divorce that can't be completed soon enough. Looking at you, the potential savior/home-buyer, the seller will almost squeeze out a tear at the thought of leaving their unfinished dream home. The listing screams, "Seller's loss is your gain!"

"Fix and Flip" home shows featuring a full crew in a sped up clip of happy hassle free drywall installation is not the actual time lapse you will experience. Tasks like ripping out old pink insulation appear to take just a few seconds without having to go back and pull off small tufts stuck to the original lumber.

Those of you who have done hardcore home renovations have probably stumbled onto abandoned toilet bowls with a drowned mouse and other unsightly headaches. HGTV leaves these parts out. They have to make it look easy because home stores are sponsors and they want you to get motivated about drywall and nail guns. It's always great to have enthusiastic friends that can tile showers and re-vamp out of code wiring on the fly for the cost of a pizza.

Of course, fire sales, with a discerning eye can make for a good investment. You find yourself visiting the same house again, this time looking around and as if possessed you hear yourself mutter, "The place has good bones." Like falling in love, becoming smitten over a specific property leads to light conversations about how easy it would be to rip out that one wall even though you've never done that sort of thing before. The real estate agent smiles and quickly agrees with your lapse of reason. Right now, you're in love, your hands are still clean and your wallet is still intact.

JES MÁRQUEZ

STATE OF THE ART

I'll always remember Brother Brian at my now defunct, bankrupt College of Santa Fe and its "state of the art" tennis center. It is now the double defunct Santa Fe University of Art and Design, still with tennis center. The students never did get a student union building, but the old farts of Santa Fe flocked to the tennis center. Now I've learned a lot from old farts and in fact, some of them are my best friends, but it seems wrong to have student loans from a college that went bankrupt.

In Brother Brian's philosophy class we discussed the horrors of today's vernacular American English, which has resulted in the overuse of the word "awesome." In human history, the word "awesome" actually translated to inspiring awe. Now diluted into the venacular it merely means, "This coffee is awesome." Travelling overseas the word "awesome" also denotes Americans are in the vicinity.

"Awesome" parallels "state of the art." The latter conjures up clean lines, stainless steel appliances and the Starship Enterprise. Applied to a New Mexico home this translates to radiant heat and a six burner gas stoves that practically does the cooking for you. A heated garage definitely belongs in the state of the art category. However, a shed/garage converted into a workshop/studio/mother-in-law suite may or may not match up with the quaint description.

Real estate agents only use the word "awesome" to describe views. When it comes to amenities, those are "state of the art" even if the appliances are broken and the house is drafty. Whatever off the grid system is included with a property is naturally, for sale purposes, state of the art. "A couple years ago" correlates with the invention of the golf cart. You will also hear the term "modern solar" which appeals more to the Hipster-Friendly-Planet-Vibe folks than the luxury country club golfers.

Utilities Nearby

On the topic of living a life of luxury, how you travel correlates to how you will adapt to your off-grid world. There are pre-packaged cruises and then there are backpackers. Having "gone on safari" does not necessarily make you a good candidate for roughing it. Staying in a fancy tent with room service and five star meals may have occurred, but while you sat in a camp chair and marveled at the starry skies, the guide and several staff members built the fire you enjoyed. After the experience some blogger goes back to an ugly big city and writes a HuffPost about how nice it was to get the whole family away from technology.

If you're the type that can eat a durian fruit without flinching you've already mastered the experiential side of life. Say you downsize so that all your clothes fit in one gym bag like the vanlifers and digital nomads. Someone who truly travels light never needs to check a bag when she flies around the world. I'm not talking about the person stuffing their cavernous four-wheel roller bag into the overhead bin. I'm talking about honest minimalists, the people that own just two pairs of underwear—one to wear, one to wash.

Cleaning out your underwear drawer is an important step in preparing yourself for life off the grid. You must be able to approach the two pairs of underwear philosophy before you start looking at solar panels. Begin forging into the off-grid river, start by doing small achievable things like making your own toothpaste. It's no different than preparing one's self for the Lets-Go-Running-Through-The-Sahara-Desert-Marathon. Sure, it seems like buying running shorts made from state of the art fabric is a critical component to preparation, but more likely you just need to start walking in the ugly shorts you already have. Walking right now is a good idea. Even with a state of the art/modern solar set up, you'll need a certain level of fitness to maintain your self-created electricity supply.

Cram your brain with survival hacks and collect the entire Foxfire books series. With Foxfire I learned about the application of chinking an Appalachian log cabin even though it's not something I've ever done. Although, I found this late night reading somewhat desperate, the skill sets from Foxfire do ensure survival. I just couldn't wrap my head around boiling lye and bacon fat to make soap. Thus, I'm back to being a poser when it comes to self-reliance. While I am hippie enough to make my own toothpaste, there's only so much time in a day for all those off-grid life chores. I still purchase my soap at the store. Sitting in my bathtub, I attempt to read the insanely small quotes on the Dr. Bronner's castile soap bottles.

A LITTLE ABOUT WATER

"Wells in the area or haul your own water!"
-Taos County Property Listing

In some Santa Fe restrooms you'll see a sign next to "Employees must wash hands before returning to work." It's the high desert alert, "This is the desert, save water, every water drop counts." Occasionally, there's also an instructional diagram on how to wash your hands correctly: suds your hands with an abrasive anti-bacterial soap, really digging in between your fingers while flushing with hot running water for several minutes. Apply hand sanitizer and use a paper towel to open the door on the way out. I walk away confused. Should I forgo using the hand-washing basin all together in an effort to conserve water while smugly reaching for the hand toweletts in my back pocket?

Humans as a species marvel at how our bodies are composed of mostly water. In survivalist terms water comes after oxygen, but before shelter and food. We can survive three minutes without oxygen, three days without water and three weeks without food. If you survive more than three days wandering without water in the desert you are either crazy or lucky. That's not an experience I want to go through.

 Having access to clean water is supposed to be one of the merits of living in the first world. Yet, here in New Mexico, "hauling water" is sometimes touted as a reasonable option when buying raw land. In the spirit of off-grid self-reliance, it seems an unwise use of my energy to haul water jugs when that time can be judiciously spent chopping fire word, working in the vegetable garden or knitting a sweater with the fur I brushed off of a Great Pyrenees dog. When making water calculations for living with a rain barrel, remember that during winter's cold snaps it's a good idea to leave the faucet running just slightly to avoid frozen pipes in northern New Mexico. Many people who want to live off-grid, usually desire basic water plumbing if at all possible. It makes everyday life so much easier.

 I'm willing to haul water on a day hike or camping trip (even an extended camping trip), but not for everyday living. I once had an acquaintance that insisted on hiking without water. She didn't want to be burdened with carrying one measly water bottle. On this particular day it was a simple trek to the top of Atalaya Trail in Santa Fe. Theoretically this is nothing hardcore unless you are a tourist coming from sea level. In the parking lot I asked her, "What about water for the dogs?" "Oh," she said, "They'll be fine." Maybe I sound like a helicopter dog parent, but I wouldn't take kids hiking and be the adult advocating, "Let's all leave our water bottles in the car so we don't have to carry them."

 It was the one time I ever hiked with this Minimalism-Becomes-A-Detriment-Woman. Maybe she just never read the latest edition of Over the Edge: Death in the Grand Canyon. Every year people have to be reminded about the basic rule of carrying water when they hike into Grand Canyon. That day on Atalaya Trail we reached the top and just thinking about how my hiking companion had no water made me thirsty. I gulped my own water and enjoyed the views. I had hiked this trail many times before. Having ample water supplies is a cardinal rule of preventing a Darwin Award. Writing this section is making me so thirsty I'm going to my kitchen for a glass of water.

Now that I'm fully hydrated, I'm reminded of another friend who has never owned a sleeping bag or learned how to fold a cowboy bedroll. She edges on the philosophy of "breatharian," which to me seems like a euphemism for martyr. The idea of the breatharian is a shoddy concept about being enlightened enough to absorb all of life's necessary nutrients by sitting in the sun and simply breathing. These people allegedly don't eat food. Such a philosophy doesn't sound like my kind of party or even a plausible concept.

My friend is not actually a breatharian, she once ate pineapple curry in front of me. I'm just astounded to know someone who honestly hardly drinks water, not even coffee. When she spontaneously headed out to camp alone, I offered to loan her a six-gallon water jug since the place she was traveling to had no on site water and little shade. She cheerfully said she may or may not stop my house and pick up the jug. Maybe this was one of those "let nature take its course" moments. We lost touch, so I'll never know.

Living off-grid is a lot like being your own manager. It's no different than preparing for a camping trip into the backcountry or even a day hike. Common sense reduces your chance of appearing on an episode of *I Shouldn't be Alive*. Nothing soothes my evening like watching someone take three days to climb three miles out of a desert canyon with a broken leg, half a bottle of water and no jacket.

When I go camping I usually spend about two weeks putting all my items on a tarp. Sometimes I'm glad to find those emergency salty ramen noodles at the bottom of my pack. Perhaps I'm overly prepared, abiding by the concept

Utilities Nearby

"two is one, one is none," like the prepper guy that makes videos about how condoms can double as emergency water carriers.

Any moment in the wilderness without water can quickly escalate to an emergency. Historically, as we learned from *Monty Python & The Holy Grail*, (the authority on medieval facts) launching a trebuchet with a large farm animal upon the enemies' water systems befell civilizations. Well poisoning is less of an issue than no well at all. That's why it's imperative to ask questions before settling into mesa paradise.

Who needs a well when you can experience the self-sufficiency of buying all your water in containers that must be trucked in? Everyone's cowboy heroes of the past know such rationalization is completely nonsensical. Cattle drives were about getting the cattle to the next water source. Areas without water were not places to hang around. This all goes back to one of the major reasons the lots of Tres Piedras never increase in value.

Speaking of cattle, you'll have one heck of a time raising livestock on your allotted community well share/cistern back up water supply plan. One average size goat drinks two gallons of water a day, maybe more if it's hot outside and they live in New Mexico. An average cow, consumes between three and thirty gallons of water per day. Let's also remember that if we forgo having children (to save the planet) and instead have two Labradors, that's another gallon of water per day. So far I have yet to water a vegetable patch. The real minimalists will claim they don't use animals in any way so all of that extra water I'm setting aside for livestock can be replaced by growing rice fields amongst the sage brush outside of Taos.

Some folks are determined to move forward with cistern plans anyway based on, "Neighbors say their water catchment system works great." This kind of generalized reassurance comforts those who will stop at nothing to get to a mesa in northern New Mexico. The rational mind concludes that since you won't ever be flushing a traditional toilet again, you'll already be saving a lot of water. Plenty of infographics tout the shocking horrors of water hog flushing commodes. When you start lugging water containers, even the low flow toilets seem wasteful. You can say you don't need a septic system because you have a composting toilet, thus you've saved water and land development costs. Everything is going swimmingly.

Perhaps I'm too practical, but having a cistern does require forethought, maintenance and time. It will be one more chore in your off-grid life when you move to an ethereal square patch of land in the desert. You're going to have to actually plan and install a water catchment system before you even get to putting a cistern in the ground or just letting it bake in the desert sun above ground. Both options require barriers—start with a minimal amount of basic screen mesh to prevent birds, rodents, lizards, snakes, scorpions and stink bugs from dying or relieving themselves into your potable water supply.

You'll need a "keep out" sign to prevent algae, bacteria, microbes and slime in your stagnant potable water supply. Invest in a filtration system and keep your catchment area free of debris. There are fancy filtration systems such as the UV light variety. I used a portable version on a camping trip and never got giardia even though the water I drank was murky brown and I was in Africa.

Someone will now write to me and explain how adding the occasional splash of household bleach keeps their cistern sanitary. Stop at the swimming pool supply store and pick up those little water pH kits so you can get out there and monitor your cistern water. If you're not wasting your life watching the reboot of *MacGyver* you'll have plenty of time to keep your cistern in top form. These are the types of decisions people are talking about when they make pithy comments about how "life is full of choices."

Utilities Nearby

If you're wedged between a rock and a hard place when it comes to water, investigate the ancient art of divining rods and forget that whole cistern plan. Whether hocus-pocus or Farmers' Almanac resurrected Grandpa who grew up in the Dust Bowl and mastered this art as a six year old, divining rods are still used today. Sometimes called a dowsing stick or water dowser, well witch strategy employs a lucky wooden forked stick (or two sticks) found in the woods or copper L-shaped rods purchased online.

There are believers and skeptics when it comes to dowsing practices. Some claim certain types of wood to be superior, others say it is the dowsing expert who has an innate knack for finding water, and naysayers call dowsing a coincidence or codswallop.

The strategy is to meander around your plot of land holding the stick and when it distinctly bends toward the ground, you've discovered the most auspicious location for your well. Logically to me, it seems reading the landscape has some merit, as for the divining rod's capabilities, give me a call. I want to witness this skill in action.

I'm surprised divining rods aren't considered a form of gambling. Wells in New Mexico can get pricey digging several hundred feet into the earth; hence the plethora of available raw land just waiting for the Self-starter/Misanthropic/End Times/Earth Lover. Better to look up at the Milky Way and pretend everything's fine. Perhaps in the long run getting that well is truly worth the investment compared with burying a bunch of giant plastic containers in the ground. You'll also want to make sure those water containers are both bullet and rodent teeth proof.

Living in nature can destroy you in the same way living in New York City can. If hantavirus and plague didn't dissolve your New Mexico fantasy, the vendetta of the rodents around here should. They can eat through Rubber Maid brand name bins leaving turds and urine in their wake.

What you think is tough plastic may still fall victim to mice and brutal New Mexico sun, wind, heat and cold. This is one more facet to consider when coming up with your water plan.

Think twice before stuffing a plastic cistern in the ground and gloating, "There, I'm finally master of the universe." Remember all the dehydrated cowboys who have sung the western classic, Cool Water. A well makes sense for pessimistic/optimistic and/or apocalyptic times, especially one that works without an electric pump. Of course, your well could go dry and you could be struck by lightning. But just like deciding which vitamins to buy, carefully consider whether or not you'll do fine with a rain barrel as a water source.

HEATING: BABY, IT'S COLD OUTSIDE

Imagining the old west romance of historic cattle drives are pure fantasy. Cowboys earned meager pay, worked to exhaustion, and sweated or froze depending on the extreme weather conditions. Cowboys sleeping under the stars on the cattle drives had small fires. Less fuel, less energy and maybe a little more sleep. With the job at hand no one had extra time to experiment with long log burning fires verses the traditional crisscross of split wood. The objective was to get the cattle to the train station while eating beans and tortillas the entire way, a la *Red River*, starring John Wayne.

Bow drill fires are theoretically a miracle fire starter option. In practice this tinder spark starting method turns out to burn a lot of calories and the results are often tiring, cold and fruitless.

Practice this skill at one of those "Mountain Men" festivals and if you can't get it, just remember to bring plenty of matches and a tea candle. Learning to start a fire with nothing but two sticks and a dream is worth pursuing prior to arriving on a remote mesa. If you're not breaking a sweat while mastering the ancient bow and drill fire, you probably cheated and pulled out your handy BBQ clicker lighter.

The bulk consumption of residential electricity goes to heating your home except for the states that still rely heavily on coal. Blogs romanticize the rediscovered concept of burning wood for warmth, "We have plenty of free wood on our land." Just exactly what kind of gentleman's Christmas tree farm or lumber operation you are running will impact your achievement in manufacturing a tropical heat wave during a blizzard.

Primal wilderness dwellers still get online to write about their energy efficient abode, how they get through sub-zero temperatures on a half cord of wood and everyone drank cocoa in their underwear. Others mention the discovery of Craiglist's "Free" section and how plenty of folks are giving away firewood. In my experience, ads of this caliber usually depict a photograph of a giant half dead tree awaiting a person with a chainsaw to come and get it.

Anyone who's paid for the trimming of looming tree branches knows that tree removal is not cheap. But on Craigslist we have a true salesman hawking his self-interest in tree removal as convenient firewood "free" for the taking. I could dovetail into a tangent on curb alert sofas, but lets just say, anything someone else is giving away that requires a large saw, manual labor, and a truck to haul is not exactly free. That's called sweat equity, which to some tree huggers translates to "free."

Living off the grid means you'd better comprehend slow burn vs. fast burn and green wood from dead wood. Pine burns faster than oak. Cedar gives ambiance with that crackling fire sound. The guys on Thieves Row by Harry's Roadhouse on Old Las Vegas Highway know what I'm talking about. A cord of wood is a cord of wood. Some folks don't know what a cord of wood actually means. My first seven winters of life were spent in Idaho and I walked to school in snows drifts taller than me so I'm aware that a cord of wood is 8 feet x 4 feet x 4 feet deep. Anything less is a half cord.

A cord of wood brings me back to the concept of chopping free firewood on your own land. With a small cabin you can probably get by sawing away on nearby dead wood. But if you live off-grid in the incongruent nature lover's 3000 square foot Earthship hacienda forget the idea that you'll hack heating with a few logs on the fire. There's a balance point between living in the square footage of a portable toilet and a sprawling castle made of automobile tires.

Unless you want to spend hours chopping wood and stoking multiple woodstoves and kiva fireplaces, going off-grid and doing it well means living in a smaller house. Remember that after all that wood chopping you need to stack it, preferably slightly off the ground. That's to stop the giant plague ridden wood rats from moving in.

In your happily ever after off-grid New Mexico life, don't get skimpy on insulation. Duct tapping Styrofoam to the inside of your ceiling will be insufficient. Passive solar building should be mandatory. No house should be built in this state that doesn't take advantage of such an effective means of heating. Passive solar design is the only source of heat that is "free" next to orienting your home around a stone hearth that kicks back heat on cloudy days.

Passive solar does require common sense (i.e. more southern exposure) in orienting a home. This means not building your garage on the southeastern corner of your abode. I've stayed in such a house and it drove me crazy how dark the kitchen was in the morning.

Outside was another spectacular New Mexico morning with the sun beating down on the southern exposure of the garage and a recessed south facing solid wood front door. The home was relatively new and built by an oblivious architect who oriented all the living spaces for views to the north. When in doubt, a beautiful view while prepping food in your gourmet kitchen is less important than southern exposure!

Coming in under budget means you're going to split some wood to keep a fire going. This will take away time from other activities such as Taco Tuesdays. Ideally you'll chop enough wood to fill an entire bedroom. That will definitely get you through the winter. It's no different than buying toilet paper in bulk because it's convenient, cheaper and you dislike going to the store.

When people tell you they built a home for practically nothing, remain skeptical. Someone somewhere cut a lot of corners or they left some expenses off the books. Just like filmmaking, you as a viewer are missing the logistics side. Ask an on set electrician. Be smitten but hold onto a wisp of trepidation. Get caught up writing the great American novel and find your fire died a few hours ago. When it's just you in a tiny cabin, re-igniting a fire will be no big deal.

Motivated people dig deeper into their dream than the armchair fence post digger. They start comparing the benefits of traditional woodstoves vs. pellet stoves. Soon there are questions about kerosene and propane. The necessity of having a woodstove for off-grid living is no joke. It's the most basic heating element and also one of the few heat sources readily available to any northern New Mexico off-grid home. Keep it stoked and you'll have rock hard muscled arms that can throw an axe like Paul Bunyan.

You're going to need a lot of wood, but it works. Admit that you're not treading as lightly on the earth as you originally intended, but thinning the forest is what keeps it healthy. Plus with all that forest thinning, you're helping Smoky the Bear prevent forest fires.

Pellet stoves make an efficient alternative, especially if throwing logs like Paul Bunyan isn't your physical calling. Pellets are a smart biofuel invention of the lumber trade. Watch out for electric blowers if the power goes out, there goes your self-sufficient heating grid. Living off-grid, you'll do better to track down the fancy pellet stoves that don't utilize an electric blower. There are a few models, like the heat-propelled fans. I just don't get a commission. If a pellet stove is your only heat source, you'll be funneling forty-pound bags of pellets into your stove faster than a rabid guinea pig can eat. Of course, that won't be everyday because this is the southwest where the sun shines.

For the individual that shuns all store bought products, you probably won't go with pellets. I doubt you'll have time in the wild to press your hand-sawed shavings into pellets. You could always build a hearth from scratch and forego a manufactured woodstove. Even with a large masonry fireplace, you'll probably still want a woodstove for the other half of the house because it's more efficient and easier to maintain on cold cloudy days.

Another option surrounding off-grid heating are "blue flame" heaters, which are a euphemism for propane (sometimes natural gas). Whoever came up with this really aced their marketing class and once caught a glimpse of a pilot light. The name "blue flame" makes it seem as if you're using a scant amount of fossil fuel. This naturally varies depending upon how cold you are and how well you built your house. Blue flame heaters are ventless wall mount heaters that in most parts of off-grid New Mexico, typically run on propane. For a small home they do work, but they cost fuel, albeit it is a seasonal expense.

One caveat on ventless blue flame heaters is that if you've barricaded yourself inside your house by sealing drafty windows and doors with plastic your ODS (Oxygen Depletion Sensor) will be triggered. That means the heater will turn off. Essentially you freeze to death (your own fault) rather than dying from carbon monoxide poisoning (the manufacturer's fault). Manufacturers will inform you that it's prudent to open a window or door periodically while the heater is running. Why anyone would want to crack open a window or door and watch their heat and

Utilities Nearby

money fly out makes me a tough sell. However, air circulation may save your life.

Concerning these charming "blue flame" heaters, I'll make one plug for the propane companies: In small cabins, in very remote places, I can see using one as a back up to a woodstove. Perhaps you just arrived and want to take the chill off while preparing the woodstove. Maybe you want the convenience of boiling water without needing to build a real log fire.

However, this starts to cancel out that whole "live for free" theory because you've got to keep that propane tank filled. Also consider that living on "Natural Splendor Lane" your muddy mountain road may not be propane truck friendly. Life in an extreme location means it costs the service truck more to reach your house. That's why watermelons and avocados in Alaska cost so much. It's the same reason "challenging build lots" are so much cheaper, like the vertical face jungle plots in Hawaii and the acre that is "mostly arroyo."

In the same shopping area as blue flame wall heaters, you'll find infrared wall heaters. Huddle around an infrared heater, close your eyes and it's as if you're standing in front of a real fire. Keep your AA batteries fresh so you can push a button to ignite it and start burning some gas. Optional electric blowers won't work off-grid and it's a good idea to keep those flammable velvet curtains a few feet away from where your wall heater is installed.

Be prudent and keep a close eye on an infrared heater, like those recipes for popovers that require heating your oven to 500 degrees Fahrenheit. Since I was a witch in my past life, infrared heaters tend to freak me out. Perhaps a reminder to me that once upon a time I was burned at the stake, probably for my foul mouth and letters to the editor.

The coziest form of heat in a New Mexico home, aside from a sunny cold day with free passive solar heating, are radiant heat floors. Thanks to all those years I spent pet sitting around Santa Fe, I can vouch for the über comfort of radiant floor heat. With a fire in the kiva and radiant floor heat, you can spend the winter rolling around naked on a sheepskin rug.

However, implementing a radiant heat system off the grid requires a high energy load at the time of year when your solar energy system is taxed the most. It can also be expensive to repair since the snaked tubing runs beneath your floors. At the time of this writing, big south ern exposure windows on sunny days heat up brick floors for far less hassle and cost.

Less glamorous, yet worth a brief mention are kerosene heaters. Old school kerosene heaters are portable, similar to the electric space heater you can't use off-grid. With kerosene heaters you have the same fresh air concerns as with other fossil fuel heat sources. Manly men use them in workshops and garages. The important precaution is to not fall asleep in a small room with a kerosene heater. Manufacturers will often state "supplemental" or "great for emergency power outages." It reminds me of when breakfast cereals were advertised as, "part of a complete breakfast."

The main inconvenience with virtually every off-grid home heating option is that you can only employ them when you are home. For energy savers this seems obvious. Aside from pure passive solar heat gain, there is no foolproof heat source. It makes weak people tempted to hold fast to their thermostat. With a low risk of fire or gas poisoning, the thermostat only requires the user to lift a finger rather than an axe or sober reasoning. The latter choices (plus coal) worked for people a century ago, so toughen up and let's talk about BTUs.

BTUs (British Thermal Units) equate to how fast your face roasts in front of the fire or more specifically, how much out put it takes to heat one pound of water by one degree. Most of off-grid northern New Mexico homes fall into climate Zone 4, translating into about 45 BTUs per

Utilities Nearby

square foot. Logically, the smaller your home, the fewer BTUs required to heat your living space. People leading the contemplative life can get by with a generous home square footage of 400 square feet. They will need a blue flame heater or stove that can churn out at least 20,000 BTUs. You might be comfortable with less. I like to over estimate (a little) on BTU's because I figure ratings are over zealous in the same way sleeping bags aren't as warm as their manufacturer rating.

Just because a heater looks like a monolithic bad ass doesn't mean it works efficiently. Think vented propane heaters. Good woodstoves and pellet stoves aren't cheap, but the investment will last years. Propane tanks run out and need to be refilled. There's the smell that isn't that bad and actually that smell is what will save your life from carbon monoxide poisoning. The real independent types settle on wood and cow pies for fuel because it's the only fuel you can harvest with your own bare hands. Just wondering, if you do use cow pies for fuel can you still call yourself a vegan?

Some of the hardcore outdoors folks might say, "Just shut up and put on a sweater when it's cold out" or "If you cared about the future of the planet you would be saving energy and you wouldn't be walking around your house naked in the winter anyway." There are people who pride themselves on the money saved by keeping the thermostat turned down or living with a simple woodstove and wearing four sweaters. Layering for winter is a relatively obvious seasonal event.

Since a few people still need the warning about not ironing a shirt while wearing it, let's touch on what layering for warmth means: When the REI store opened in Santa Fe I swore I would not shop there. It wasn't even adobe. But I was showing a new to Santa Fe friend around town and we joined in on the Snow Shoeing Seminar. My new friend in her forties looked around the room and wondered if she'd stepped into a retirement club. She whispered, "Jes, everyone here is old." I was still in my fleeting twenties and said, "Duh, it's Santa Fe." One woman made notes on a cat themed note pad. Another attendee commented, "But it's cold." That's when the lecturer pointed to the mannequin decked out in REI jackets at the front of the room, "That's why we layer up." His arm motioned toward the base layers on the mannequin. Seminar attendees seemed confused and the energy in the room let out a cough. Under those florescent lights, the Santa Fe baby boomers were losing interest in snow shoeing just thinking about the possibility of being cold.

It makes me wonder about that whole San Luis Valley of Colorado. One reader informed me that he knew many off-grid folks who lived through the winter in this area. Yes, the Reed family finally made it out of the Sierra Nevada after the winter of 1846, but they barely made it. Surviving and thriving mean different things to different people.

Cold weather junkies don't care for hot steamy summer nights. A bubbly friend of mine once invited me on a winter camp out. She herself had actually never spent one night in a tent. When I asked if she had warm winter boots, she said "No." When I told her it would be very cold she said, "That's just part of the experience."

Living off-grid will expose you to the elements. Weather has always been a part of life on grid or off, but now weather dictates more of your life experience. Heating a house is not such a big deal if you live in Hawaii or any cliché location of equatorial summer bliss. In this trade in for the tropics, you won't worry about heat, yet those rainforest clouds will cut into your available solar electricity. This information is relevant to the person moonlighting as a Reiki master at the Zen Center, but who has dreams of starting a vegetable garden/retreat center in Hawaii.

Solar panels will provide electricity but they are not (currently) well suited to heating your home and that's why

UTILITIES NEARBY

every technical analysis brings us back to logs and cow pies. This is the self-sufficient western experience. Of course, if you can access geothermal or hydro-electricity you're fortunate and have even more options than the average soul. Remember fake fireplaces and digital crackling fire sounds have no bearing in the self-reliant world.

READERS' COMMENTS

Truly great post! Wait question! Why can't you drink the water in Cerrillos and Madrid? I knew the water table was messed up and thought that was why everyone had water holding- what's wrong with the water there? I just bought land outside El Rito. Anything I'm supposed to know? I'll pay you to tell me. It has the Valecitos river on it and lots of grass. You guys can come up and camp for free if you want.

-Anonymous

This is crucial, eye-opening information for me. I am looking to buy an Earthship and there are some good caveats listed here. Thank you for putting forth the effort in write this expose', it is a valuable post!

-Anonymous

Thanks for the post. I am new to NM and I found this very helpful and witty ;). I lived my first month "off-grid" on the Mesa in Taos and was so enchanted the first 10 days. That wore off quickly with the rocky mile long driveway that was killing my car, the insane amounts of dust, Monsoon season coming and quickly figuring out the $$ on propane if I were to stay (lived there in June so not such a bad month just as your article states). Moved into town in July and couldn't be happier. Little apartment all utilities included. Can walk everywhere. One thing I will say about the Mesa is that it's really beautiful out there. But I agree with you, it would make much more sense to own than rent. Thanks for the info! You have a good sense of humor as well.

-Elisa

Utilities Nearby

Thanks for the heads up ... I did live in a solar house outside of Madrid which I had to go around turning things off just to turn on other things ... it had a bathroom and good enough water from a little water tower. I am thinking of moving to Taos ... the Earthships sound kind of neat.

-Jean

What prevents the rattlers from following the mice down the chimney in a non off-grid house? I really want to know, as I am considering rural living, after 4 decades in Santa Fe. Thx for your info!

-Anonymous

Thank you so much for your warnings........so informative. All renters should shout out warnings to help others.... question. what is it about the water in Madrid and Cerrillos ...does that apply to Galisteo?

Thank You,
Carole

Hi Jes,
I found your old emails! What a hoot. How is ABQ treating you? I am living in Abiquiu - King Pin of Odd Balls & Haters. Huge old gold mine right on Chama Rio about a mile north of Bode's market. There are 2 farms that grow right along that stretch using river water, those farmers are mad as hatters, one quit doing Santa Fe Farmer's Market (I think they were banned actually for scaring customers), other is limping along - hurray!

Anyway, my point is mercury is rampant in NM water. Good RO will pull it out...I NEED TO MOVE. I want a nice house (unfurnished!) with land to keep neighbors back! Willing to look anywhere in NM, since Santa Fe looking has been bust. I have great credit, no pets, can spend up to $2,000, need long term..... sooner better. I PAY FINDERS FEE!!!!!!!!

Cheers,
Mark

Thanks so much -- I am pretty much a spiritual yuppie (is that even a term? LOL) who wants to live with a lot of privacy and clean air and water. I'm a corporate trainer and former investigative reporter who also is a bit woo-woo. I like my creature comforts (although I made it through 4 days with no potable water and had to boil the water from a neighbor's swimming pool and then pick out the mosquitoes) and being snowed in for 4 days and for having no electricity for 3 days... but 9 days is a very long time, especially when you are sick.

-Anonymous

Hi,

I saw your post on Craigslist, and was wondering if you would be willing to email back and forth a bit, to answer some questions about off-grid living in Taos vicinity? My sister is looking to move to Tres Piedras. While she's not looking to rent, she is looking to bring her tiny house, a cat, and a dog. She is also wanting to get a plot of land there for our mother, who is a senior. It would be her first time trying to live off the grid, and she has several concerns similar to some of those that you mentioned in your ad. She's wanting a more realistic look at some of the struggles that can occur. For example, she has questions about what it is realistically like to try and live in Tres Piedras or Carson Estates, whether it's safe for a single woman and animals (she'd be

Utilities Nearby

leaving her animals unattended during the day as she'd be working), how difficult it is to live off of solar there in the winter, realistically what the climate is like, issues getting water, etc. I know you mentioned some of this in your email, but I was wondering if you'd be willing to go into a little more detail and answer some more specific questions? If so, let me know, I'll relay some questions. If not, no worries at all, thank you for the informative post, and have a great day! Thanks!

-Julie

I'm a veteran with a stable monthly pension and burned out on CA living. I'm looking for alternative housing options like off-grid or caretaker and saw your awesome ad. Thanks! Getting good intel is insanely difficult these days. Even here in Desert Hot Springs, CA and trying to find straight forward info about homesteading in the desert is almost impossible. I have a small pension. Any ideas?

Thanks,
Scott

Great ideas, thanks! I love the National Parks idea!
Thanks again, Scott

Very entertaining indeed! Thank you for sharing :) I live in the urban hell of northern California, I'm putting together a little nest egg to move to NM, spring 2018, will be building an off-grid place on my acre in Abiquiu, do you know of any good builders? Going for a 350 sq ft studio with sleeping loft, electric on the property :) will be doing catchment, neighbors are quite successful with it. Thanks!

-Catherine

Thanks, although I lived in Santa Fe for years I do confess, being a New Englander I was bewitched by the lure of Earthships and the fantasy of living off the grid. Thanks!

-Anonymous

Thank you for your warning. Very informative and very much appreciated. You are definitely speaking to me, because I am currently in Maryland and want to escape the crappy, unhealthy rentals that seem to be everywhere these days and hoped that at least the "off-grid" places would be better. I've been reading all I can to learn how to do an off-grid lifestyle for myself, so really appreciate and get your very informative details. Thank you so much!
I've also thought it interesting how, after the incredible amount of time, money, and effort it took someone to create an off-grid home why they don't live there themselves. So now I know why. Thanks so much and keep posting.
-N
Really excellent advice. Thanks for taking the time to post all this ... Are you in rentals?
Real estate is your calling.

-Nick

Thanks for this. The million dollar Earthship I rented, was full of rattlesnakes, they crawled around at night. I lived in my car here for 30 years, up there, my friends at the Pueblo, saw where I was living, very fancy, and their eyes bugged out, they said do not stay in here at night, they showed me how the rattles followed the mice, even down the chimney. Then they left. Million dollar badly built Earthship and I'm sleeping in the truck, many thieves prey on us.

Blessings
-Michael

U R GREAT! Thank you so so much! I lived in my car here for 25 years, a true American experience. Keep up the great work, my book is mostly written, but my health is failing due to exposure, I want to edit it, I will give you half, it's called ten thousand nights on the road! New agers, boomer, old breed son! Let me know! Thanks

-Michael

Subject: Large Clear Lemurian Seed Quartz Natural Point Cluster Crystal Rough Healing | eBay

Hi, sorry forgot your name. I'm Mark. Remember me maybe?
Anyway you wrote, "Bonus Info: If you are new to New Mexico, understand that you can NOT drink the water near Madrid/Cerillos. You cannot cook pasta in it either. Forget it."

Can you elaborate on this, since I am looking at a few rentals in that area? Is e-coli in water or what makes is dangerous? You know you absorb up to a liter, when you shower?

Thank you! Mark

Whoever you are, I could not agree MORE! And stay away from the Greater Earthship subdivision (I REFUSE to call it a community; they haven't a clue what that means). The solar batteries (6, I think; the caretaker waters them) store NOTHING! I had to buy a frigging generator, which I guess I'll be using again today. I can't believe my landlords think they're going to even sell this house, let alone get $200,000 for it. Even with a kiva, I am freezing in subzero temps because the damn thing blows the smoke back into the house, so I have to put it out while I'm being poisoned by the smoke. The landlords' caretaker (ahem) said the blowback is natural. Nothing he can do. Not that he told the landlords to maybe call a freaking chimney sweep or anything like that. Landlords are sloughing off all the costs of their ill-conceived homes onto the tenants.

I'll be leaving on March 20. Don't think with the endless (well...) snow and moisture that I'll be able to get to my little quarter-acre on the mesa by then (can't grade the land or lay down the prefab cabin), so I'm not sure what my living situation will be. Just glad, overall, that it will not be in "Hippiecrite Ville."

Thanks for posting!

-J

P.S. An anecdote: during the heavy rains in Autumn (or was it August?), half of the one road in and out of this subdivision caved in (maybe 20 ft. deep by 20 ft. wide). The other half was dicey, to say the least. I commented to everyone and on the GWC FB page that perhaps the people in Guatemala could have a fundraiser for us so that we could get the road fixed. It took 21 days, and someone had the nerve to say, "You should see how long it took to fix the other side when that went out last year." Really? Way to set the bar low. Why bother having one when it's already at ground level. What an AWFUL experience.

Hello: First, I would like to say that it was really thoughtful of you to post this. I have lived in NM now for 7 years, coming from Los Angeles. I lived in a relatively nice place in Santa Fe the first four years. My landlord, on the other hand, was not so nice. When our well went out he wanted to wait till the weekend was over to call a plumber, leaving five houses without water for 3 days. And the landlord was a trustfunder that received over $150,000 a month. They would never fix anything without a fight and then I was basically a bitch, especially when I asked for screens for my place, which they promised upon moving in, a year and a half had passed and still no screens. Then the landlord asked me to move out because he was supposedly selling the property. He gave me 30 days to get out and ultimately never listed or sold the property.

Then I lived in Madrid, land of the stinky water. Never would have moved there if I had known about the water. So I had to haul all my water from Santa Fe, and I have goats and sheep. Even they wouldn't drink the water, if you can believe that. The tiny little miner's cabin had a propane heater, which cost me like $300 a month to use in the winter, and I only kept it at 65 degrees. Then there was the coal dust everywhere and garbage and broken glass coming out of the ground everywhere you stepped. In addition, almost everyone that lives in Madrid are total scumbags, drug addicts, drunks and thieves, except a few business owners.

Now I am in Abiquiu, which is very pretty with the river and lake close by. I do have an adobe house, but the only heat provided is a wood stove, which basically heats only one room of a three bedroom house. Everything else is electric including my well pump, so if the electricity goes out, I can't even flush the toilet. So I basically live in this one room through the winter with blankets over the doorway and windows. And then there is the drive to town, which is at least an hour. I'm not sure all the beauty is worth the inconvenience. I mean, you can always take day trips to pretty places, right?

I think your post touched upon every topic about living in these rural areas, and especially off-grid. I think if more people read it they would avoid making all these mistakes. I actually was considering buying a piece of property out here in Abiquiu because there is some really beautiful cheap land. But in many of these places you would have to haul water, use solar, propane and probably have a composting toilet. Yeahh, it would be cheap, but really inconvenient in so many ways, which you enumerated in your post. Thanks so much for posting this. I think I will stick to places with amenities even though it costs more money.

Sincerely,
-JC

Props to you for taking the time to write and share this. Sorry for whatever bummer situation prompted it.

-Anonymous

Oh my goodness!!! Thank you for your wealth of information, your time and energy in putting this together. I am moving from Virginia City to Taos. Thank you so much!!!

With warm regards,
-Marietta

omg omg THANKS SO MUCH FOR POSTING THIS ....U SAVED ME FROM MOVING TO AN OFF THE GRID CABIN...I HAD MY MIND MADE UP TO GO THERE THEN I READ YOUR POSTING ....TRUTHFULLY MY HUSBAND AND I ARE DISABLED AND ON OXYGEN AND HE IS 62 SO THANKS SO MUCH FOR THIS U CHANGED MY MIND

-Darla

Subject: Re: I love all your posts
Thank you very much for this post! You saved us from

making a huge mistake. We are new to this area and have nearly fallen prey to the sleight euphemistic taxonomy used in the off-grid rental advertisements.

- Karin

Good Morning, Thank you for your posting. I too love NM, and am thinking of moving to a more "rustic" environment. Some of the cautions I know to stay away from, such as propane. Others I will definitely research more. Thanks again, the information was a real eye opener.

Blessings to you and yours, and have a great day.

-Anonymous

Thank you for your warning. Very informative and very much appreciated.
Jeremy

A truly wonderful read, thank you for the enlightenment & wealth of knowledge! (Not sarcasm)

-Flora

Good stuff, and well written. May I make a suggestion? To promote readability, try narrowing the width of your paragraphs. Paragraphs with a width smaller than six-inches make reading much easier. Thanks for the good info.

-Jim (looking for a room in Taos)

UTILITIES NEARBY: RUSTIC RETREAT = VIRTUOUS SOULS

"Most people around here use an outhouse."

"This property could be connected to the grid but…"

"This charming property has no indoor plumbing but…"

-Property descriptions in northern New Mexico

Vagary is one of New Mexico real estate's notorious joys. Rustic cabins are "nestled" into mountain sides with "internet available." Owner built homes are constructed "with love" rather than ignorance. Homes with obvious issues are described as "one of kind" or "idiosyncratic." "Whimsical" means the home falls outside the building code. "Cozy" means the toilet and kitchen are separated by a beaded curtain, sans door. "Utilities nearby" can be anywhere from the lot line to the horizon line depending upon your personal interpretation of distance. It's all a nebulous beauty until you get a quote from the utility company that confirms just how far you really are from having it all.

Utilities Nearby

More importantly, you're going to want more than five acres to truly enjoy your mesa mountain bliss. I can tell you from experience that five acres is not enough to avoid hearing the neighbors talking about their recent colonoscopy. Maybe I couldn't actually see the neighbors, but clumps of juniper trees do not negate sound traveling over property lines. So much for being "nestled" on my own private juniper tree studded paradise.

As a single young woman, several years prior to actually moving into an off-grid rental, I checked out a place for myself. The "whimsical cabin/artist retreat" was on my dream road, winding through the trees, miles from pavement. Just driving to such a remote enclave made me giddy. Beyond the power lines there were no man made obstructions to remind me of the modern world.

I have always been leery of properties proclaiming "landlord on site." Out in the country without neighbors, the last person you want peering in at you is the landlord or the artist dude renting the other outbuilding. Even if you consider yourself to be an upstanding citizen who doesn't partake in heavy smoking, skeet shooting, loud sex, or strange solstice celebrations, it's unsettling having to pass the landlord's house and wave as your car navigates the pothole dirt road.

I met up with Kathy the landlord who lived in the main house. She escorted me to the off-grid cabin just up the hill. Kathy spoke gleefully about the mountain meadow views and the convenience of a hospital toilet in the otherwise complete bathroom. Anyone that has ever had surgery or otherwise been bed bound knows what I'm talking about. It's the hospital chair with a circle cut out in the seat, stainless steel arms and the plastic bucket underneath. The floors of the bathroom were real Saltillo tile giving that illusion of authentic New Mexico. I might have said out loud, "It's a really cute bathroom."

It reminded me of that anxiety dream where there's no toilet or you're in a public place and there's no door to the toilet and/or the toilet water is rising rapidly from a dreaded clog. The landlord discussed the hospital toilet as being "only for emergencies." Emergency translated to when it's the middle of the night and/or when it's a butt freezing cold trek to the outhouse. The latter accounts for at least half of the year in northern New Mexico. I considered how living out here, I would no longer drink tea before bed, not even kava or Nighty-Night tea.

My would-be artist retreat rental property also came with an outhouse that was ostensibly "rustic, yet fabulous." It was for the times when you have to admit you still go number two even though you are enlightened and "mostly vegan." After climbing the ladder to the sleeping loft with a ceiling the height of a hatchback car, the landlord led me to the outhouse.

Discreetly located amongst juniper trees, the outhouse was a fair distance from the cabin. I could see why the hospital toilet was positioned in the indoor bathroom. Constructed of weathered plywood, the outhouse doorway faced into the branches of a juniper tree. There was no door and upon entering, I could see toilet paper piled precariously close to the top of the pit. There was no way I would make summer without needing to tell the landlord I had a backed up outhouse that just couldn't take any more shit.

Before you assume I'm "poo-pooing'" outhouses, allow me to confirm that I've had positive experiences using an outhouse in New Mexico. It was June as I stepped toward a quaint stuccoed building with a screen door to keep the flies out. On this particular summer morning, wild flowers were in full bloom and the birds were singing.

This experience inspired me to consider an outhouse as a viable alternative to indoor plumbing. I read about how to construct a monumental outhouse and even came across a calendar celebrating the architectural diversity in outhouse

Utilities Nearby

construction. At the time, I was twenty years old and liked sarongs. It was before Birkenstocks sandals made a come back.

I had one more reservation in considering this particular "Artist Retreat" rental with outhouse because it was located within site of an outbuilding that an artist guy used occasionally. Personally, I wasn't comfortable with the idea that occasionally artist guy would see me walking to my rustic shitter just steps off the driveway. Even if I used the indoor hospital toilet, I'd have to walk outside to empty my urine filled bucket from time to time.

I don't care if my pee contributed to wonderful fertilizer. Peeing in the woods is not the same thing as paying rent to empty a hospital potty on a daily basis. Am I wrong to assume that the whole idea of being home is so you can shit in private? Maybe I'm just not the commune type.

However, I support America's National Forests by using the pit toilets during camping trips. Some of which have been sparkling clean as far as pit toilets are concerned. One morning I watched several forest rangers roll up in a truck. After emptying camper trash from the bear proof cans, one man sprayed copious amounts of sanitizer all over the bathroom and replenished the toilet paper. This particular pit toilet didn't have the giant commercial toilet paper roll the size of a hubcap. It was always restocked with one measly standard household roll, which during high season wasn't enough in the women's pit toilet. I guess it's akin to motels that don't want to tempt guests by offering extra toilet paper rolls that might be stuffed into a duffle bag.

As a side note, if you are taking toilet paper rolls out of motel rooms as a vengeful guest or just because you're a cheapskate, the world has sunk to new lows in human morality. Kept near commodes everywhere, civilizations rise and fall with the availability of cornhusks and old Sears catalogs.

Although it seemed paradoxical to watch a forest ranger using the same sanitizing sprayers hailed by Monsanto as perfectly safe, pit toilets have become an odd necessity of humanity's desire to catch a glimpse of wilderness. Nowadays pooping in the woods is almost illegal. In that moment I wasn't witnessing the sounds of nature, but the park ranger janitorial duties that were no different than the employee pushing a cleaning cart toward a crowded airport bathroom.

Harping on toilets may seem like I have some Freudian fixation, but toilets (or going behind a shrub) is something we all experience everyday. In the past, composting toilets were awkward box shaped thrones used by tree huggers and that made the flushing commode populace leery. Today there's a plethora of thrones available in the composting category, some of which look like ordinary toilets. There's still the old five-gallon bucket option, but traveling the world or living green isn't always instagram worthy.

The Japanese are the true pioneers when it comes to fancy heated toilet seats with remote control bidets. Just go use the toilet at 10,000 Waves in Santa Fe and experience what I'm talking about. It's no off-grid commode. Even if you don't have to go, you'll feel a compulsion to sit there and maybe write out your bucket list or read the latest issue of Eldorado Vistas.

In a few countries bidets are mandatory and millions can't imagine living without this everyday bathroom essential. Dr. Mercola, notable for his healthy living newsletters, decided to sell his own brand bidet attachment in the US.

The goal of modifying standard American toilets was commendable, but then being a man, Dr. Mercola added, "It's virtually eliminated the need for toilet paper in my home." Millions of women will probably disagree with this statement including myself. Particularly when you've moved in with a man who purportedly can make one roll of single ply toilet paper last an entire month.

UTILITIES NEARBY

While bidet-loving nations look down at dirty Americans with our copious toilet paper usage, the necessity for a bidet is debatable. With a burning desire to live off-grid, you probably have survived life up to this point without a bidet, especially if you're an American. My point is that in choosing off-grid living, you're at the crossroads of nature or a Hammacher Schlemmer catalog.

I read somewhere that good outhouses begin with a three-foot wide hole dug six-feet deep. Historically, the buildings were traditionally temporary or abandoned once the pit was out of order. Then a new pit would be dug and the building would be moved over the new hole in the ground. The iconic half moon symbol cut out in the door meant it was a ladies toilet, although this is speculation. Dedicated men's toilets never lasted long and thus apparently, none have survived. Some outhouses had no decorative ventilation. Half moon symbol or not, you'll be surprised by the prevalence of outhouse friendly real estate lurking in northern New Mexico.

Here's a treasured example:

Off-grid solar cabin property 25 minutes from Taos. No neighbors and close to the Petaca canyon and other excellent rugged wild hiking. The 500 square foot cabin is on a half acre with a mobile home and double seat out house.

These are the places that make me love northern New Mexico and it beats an apartment in the city. A double seat outhouse makes me feel like a gold prospector. I wonder who my lucky outhouse mate will be? It would be far more useful to know the date the outhouse was built and it's occupant frequency. These essential statistics would help potential buyers assess required maintenance. It's similar to knowing when the roof was last replaced.

Before I receive backlash from the hippies, I want to mention the merits of the outhouse: Given the choice between living with an HOA offering indoor plumbing and an outhouse with no bylaws, I will always choose the outhouse, even when it's snowing. But just because "Most people in the area use an outhouse," does that mean you should follow the trend too?

In the same vein as theoretical amenities, New Mexico real estate sometimes mention theoretical energy options in off-grid listings. You'll read it as a blip of possibility. For example, "harness the wind" sounds like inspirational wall art bought in the deep discount bin of Hobby Lobby. The person making this suggestion has no intent to actually "harness the wind" at his own home. It's written by a real estate agent who lives in a Santa Fe condo, or a FSBO (for-sale-by-owner) who can no longer be bothered with energy experimentation.

Wind energy seems like a simple concept, especially during New Mexico's spring season when breezy days are typical. But when a house has an abandoned would be wind turbine, that's a red flag. I'm talking about turbines without the turbine, an obelisk amongst sagebrush. We're talking about purchasing a New Mexico property that comes with a small version of the Washington Monument. The turbine ruins suggest that whoever lived in the house prior to you failed at harnessing the wind.

Wind energy is like the old days of solar where students at MIT sought to bottle summer heat for winter warmth. It's such a logical theory, yet physics pre-empts current technology. Producing energy is very doable, it's storing that energy for later usage that poses a complex challenge for solar and wind to be adopted on a universal scale. Like solar, wind is a one hundred percent renewable resource.

The challenge is that no one can predict the wind and it's available at a constantly shifting rate. Cost is the most significant factor in harnessing the wind for an off-grid personal residence. Wind turbines can be installed as a supplemental energy source, but they once again slam the misnomer that living off-grid can be done "for free."

STUCCO SUN LOVING GODDESS

Since living in a gray stucco off-grid fiasco, I have learned a lot from our old school handyman, Ruben. Everything he builds is a perfect square. In his decades of construction he's only chopped off one finger. Visiting the city office for a permit, Ruben knows the lingo. When the administrative woman asks, "Are you the contractor?" you answer, "I'm just the handyman." This DIY on the sly style of rennovation usurp certain licensing requirements. Plus there's a little property tax break when your dwelling is in a state of perpetual, "It's not finished yet." Therefore the property is in the process of being "improved", but is not currently definable as improved.

Perpetual construction is a chronic state of being in New Mexico. Adding stucco finishing, particularly in any shade that is not New Mexico gray is an immediate tip off that you actually intend to complete your home. This sort of type-A motivation is rarely seen in off-grid built homes, but it is mandatory in the Eldorado subdivision. Cement, traditional, synthetic, no one cares as long as your stucco is done right. In your fantasies about solar community houses remember your number one red flag: pervasive New Mexico gray dwellings.

Now that I've had the opportunity to schlep and trowel a few thousand pounds of stucco, I understand what went wrong back in our off-grid rental home. When you hire a licensed stucco crew, the project gets completed in two sunny day sessions mitigating possible moisture damage. The weekender couple, on the other hand, trowels and flings stucco at a much slower rate. During such intermittent stucco sessions, how do I know Mr. Patchouli made certain his strawbales were moisture free prior to stuccoing?

Looking at a gray coat of base cement stucco, I see how a potential renter or homebuyer might fall prey to "looks fine to me." Blind to DIY builder's fatigue, you won't notice where the roof top corners received a haphazard stucco application. Simply fling stucco onto your metal hawk, now trowel over the lath. Feel the lactic acid building your arm muscles faster than you can stucco and float. With the finish coat and an obsessive-compulsive nature, I bask in the glow of truly sealed stucco. I also have a fitness level that would never be achievable in a gym.

Mixing stucco is not as romantic as stomping grapes from your personal vineyard. If you're not ready to bite the bullet and have pallets of stucco cement delivered remember that each bag of El Rey Fast Wall weighs eighty pounds and covers approximately twenty-five square feet. You have to load the bags from the store shelf to a flat bed cart, then into your truck and then you'll unload them. You'll move them one more time to throw a bag in your wheelbarrow. That's before you add water, usually about one and half gallons, or until your stucco has the consistency of elephant dung. Don't get cheap when buying a wheelbarrow. You need the extra heavy-duty type with double rugged wheels, not the single wheel garden dabbler model. For more grand projects, you'll need a cement mixer, which will need to run off a generator.

Like bellying up to the all you can eat buffet that "mostly completed" sprawling New Mexico home sure sounds like a bargain. When buying raw land without a well, you'll have to invest in a water source before you can stucco. I guess that's why some properties on the market show beautiful framed adobe walls, but unfortunately the owners are now selling before the project is complete. When you do get done with your stucco job, it's time to clean your tools and that also requires water. Do yourself a favor and build a smaller home. This isn't Texas.

WHY DO YOU TRASH STRAWBALE?

I said a few negative things about strawbale homes. Recalling the story of The Three Little Pigs, it was the first pig in the straw house that had his house blown down by the big bad wolf. Perhaps fairy tales are irrelevant but most of them have some moral code brought to light in a sinister way. After living in a strawbale home, I recognized that strawbale is not the ideal building material for homes in northern New Mexico, or any place with periodic snow or rain. More frequently than not, snow and rain falls in a diagonal line because breezeless days are a figment of imagination. A large metal roof overhang doesn't necessarily stop moisture from hitting your stuccoed walls.

Being a fan of the flexible building codes of northern New Mexico, means all sorts of structures are possible, but this does not translate to livable. You'll come across property descriptions that read, "This partial adobe home…," essentially if one wall is adobe the seller will call it an adobe home. Lost in the moment, you'll overlook the fact that there are three other walls and they are made of straw. Partial adobe home translates into, "This whole building a hacienda on the mesa thing cost a lot more than we anticipated."

Build a smaller home so that your four walls cram into a total adobe or pumice budget. Cut square footage, not materials. Traditional adobe homes were built with small windows and low ceilings making them easier to heat. Old, authentic adobe houses do not have soaring ceilings.

Strawbale structures work well for barns, carports and sheds which people do not live in, because these sorts of structure allow the wind to blow through them. During the summer in our off-grid strawbale house, when our doors were flung open all day, it didn't initially dawn on us that strawbale would be a problem. The major pit fall of strawbale, particularly for the DIY builder are cracks leading to trapped moisture. Moisture in a strawbale wall leads to mold and a structural problem. This is a difficult and costly issue. Never mind the respiratory health concerns that mysteriously appeared during our time living in a strawbale home. Neither myself, nor my spouse have asthma or emphysema. The scratchy throat syndrome disappeared after we moved out.

Strawbale homes are not the same as a well sealed home housing you from the harsh elements. During construction, one damp bale will be the bane of misery. Maybe the straw looks as if it had dried out in the New Mexico sun, but once sealed inside several layers of stucco, just wait out the clock on strawbale revenge. Thick walls that make attractive rodent habitats and lack the thermal mass of adobe are not worth the energy expended in home construction. I am sure I will get some flack for sharing my unsolicited opinion: Strawbale is the poor man's adobe.

Depending upon the visionary responsible for constructing the monstrosity you're currently living in will dictate your level of discomfort. The large overhangs necessary on a strawbale home are supposed to direct water away from the strawbale walls. This has the added effect of defeating the purpose of building a passive solar home. Eaves on a house interfere with the sun goddess philosophy of large southern exposure windows.

When you live in a house that is completely reliant on off-grid energy, a house with a roof overhang on the southern wall will always be darker and you'll want to flip on a light switch even on a sunny day. But barring limited green solar power for night-time illumination, tread cautiously when doling out electricity during daylight hours.

Many people make the initial assumption that strawbale walls are the epitome of a cozy New Mexico home. On a surface level this is true. Just looking outside through the deep window sill of a strawbale house gives the feeling of insulation.

UTILITIES NEARBY

In contrast, real adobe walls will stand the test of time. They are baked and cured by the New Mexico sun and will outlive you. Yes, traditional adobe bricks have straw in their composite, but that is secondary to the earthy thermal mass value in every authentic adobe. Go traditional and do ox-blood hardened floors. Given direct southern exposure adobe will radiate a lot more passive solar heat than a strawbale home and make living off-grid a viable option. This is why adobe is the hallmark of authentic New Mexico real estate.

A few people wrote to me to debunk my experience of the strawbale house. They said I was wrong and what a great experience they had had living in a home made of straw. Barring first class stuccoing and truly moisture free straw bales, it's plausible that a strawbale home can work for a while, but for durability and investment, it is a material more suited to courtyard walls and yard sculptures. I still trust my college instructor who built an adobe house off-grid and he's the one who said with a grimace, "Strawbale has no thermal mass."

WIFI IS FOR WEAK PEOPLE

In New Mexico, securing an internet frequency can be iffy, yet a high frequency of properties use feeble language to describe internet access without elaborating on tangible options. Only recently have signs appeared in remote areas proclaiming, "Finally! High Speed Internet Now Available in this Area."

When a property has bonafide internet access it's boldly stated as in "high speed" or "broadband." Such direct real estate lingo supports the concept that the person who wrote the property description is confident. However, broadband access means you probably aren't living like a wild woman in the woods. Broadband means you live on an acre in Eldorado.

Uncertainty is best expressed in the rental ad for an un-insulated cabin. After mentioning "serenity" the ad teeters on "internet available." Translation: "The last treehugger that lived here before you never needed internet and neither should you." This non-judgmental/kindness crowd will remind you that although you're the first tenant to ask about internet since the unveiling of AOL, it's okay. They'll be happy to put in a few wires and a satellite, just remember you'll forfeit your deposit.

Digital nomads living in the campgrounds towards San Francisco can hoist up their jet pack and for several hundred bucks a month, catch up on a little freelance work in their WiFi enabled retro camper. New Mexico is not that hip although a few fortunate properties boast "fiber optics in road." This means you're at the helm of state of the art meets wilderness.

More backwoods locations sometimes have DSL and if not, your option is a satellite internet cooperative with tech support run by volunteers. Satellite is doable, unless you're the hard core gaming type that never sees the sun and your only real social interaction is once a year when you go to the gamers' convention. Slower internet speeds may be the cost of living on your dream property. It means you might not qualify for a remote work position at Amazon. Remember that your satellite will also suck a little juice from you photovoltaic system.

Keep in mind that in New Mexico, no one is in a hurry. Internet availability will now depend on slope, trees, and mesas. "Clear line of sight and "depending on vegetation" sounds like navigating a jungle. These are factors in determining if internet coverage is in the stars for you. It's the technological revolution and New Mexico is far from the epicenter. On the bright side consider that sometimes Xfinity takes several weeks to make a home visit even to the on grid subdivisions. The latter anecdote is based on a true story.

Utilities Nearby

On my first Santa Fe County foray into remote, but on grid living I had satellite internet. The company ran a cable from a "clear line of site" position. This was a gently slopping hill several hundred yards from the house. A few days later a coyote ate through the cable since it was preliminarily installed draping over the golden grasses. Someone from installation was supposed to trench the cable, but hadn't gotten around to it. There was no need to bother with trenching because the cows in the area enjoyed using the internet station pole as a scratching post. Apparently one cow realized what a great backscratcher the internet post made and informed the other cows. The cows were winning and internet guy would have to come up with another solution. Eventually a satellite was installed with WildBlue, which worked well enough considering that it was a decade ago, the dark ages of technology.

With the right combination of money and motivation, just about anything can be accomplished. Even boondocking RV's have satellite internet. Using your phone as a hotspot would be so easy if T-mobile just put in the infrastructure in the places I love that have two people per square mile. I'm a lifetime customer. It will be worth it.

A few people will tell me to stop ranting and forget internet because it's incongruent with a life in the wild. Instead simply put on a tin foil hat, which is what some people did when the Santa Fe public libraries installed WiFi. Electromagnetic fields are another topic entirely and again, the majority of New Mexico still remains as nature intended.

HOT WATER, GRAYWATER

Few things are more miserable than running out of hot water. Climbing into a bath of tepid water when it's cold outside is technically survivable, but not enjoyable. The simple act of turning on a faucet and getting hot water is one of the most comforting inventions in the history of civilization. Hot water is a true in home luxury that is often taken for granted when readily available.

In the past, barring water born bacteria that no one knew about during the Roman Empire, traditional bathhouses of lost civilizations utilized hypocaust heating systems. The hypocaust system worked a lot like the stovetop Italian espresso maker with a furnace fire below pushing hot air upward. Without excavating a lot of ground, today's minimalists install small on demand hot water heaters and enjoy hot showers at home. For special occasions, there's the splurge on a weekend spa get away for treatments like the "soulful burrito body wrap."

Living without running water on a voluntary basis, sounds commendable, crazy or tough. Every time you want a gallon of hot water you first need to build a fire. I imagine the baths drawn for cowboys of the old west. Boiling kettles of water is a lot of work. Even boiling water in a metal oil drum (a full bath) is going to take time and fuel. This goes back to needing an axe to chop more wood.

Still maybe you're captivated by the wood fired heated wok style Filipino tubs that sit directly over a fire. If you're soaking solo, you'd better be willing to climb out naked and throw a few more logs on the fire. If you've got company, you can play rock-paper-scissors to decide who has to get out of the tub and stoke the fire. There is nothing sexier than that Neanderthal feeling. Being a realist is the bane of my existence, but the photographs of social media travel are lovely. No wonder all the natural hot springs of the mountains have been discovered, less physical labor and more hedonism. In rustic conditions, what am I supposed to do when it's cold outside and my big dog peed on my Chihuahua again?

We can be thankful for technology's gift of hot water bliss provided by portable tankless water heaters. Tankless water heaters are typically reliant on either gas or electricity

Utilities Nearby

and are not completely solar. They are often used in small, tiny homes and are incredibly affordable to purchase. Using a tankless hot water heater off-grid will be one of the reasons you don't banish the propane tank. Reduce the heater's thermostat and save! Feel lucky as you meditate on how people a century ago couldn't bathe everyday like you.

Say no to fossil fuels and you've always got the simple camper solar shower bag option. Just leave the three-gallon vinyl shower bag on the hood of your car for a couple hours and hope for a lot of sun. Even more simple is to put your garden hose in the sun. The heated water, albeit limited, is absolutely free with zero emissions. Then again, when lightening your load on a camping trip, do you really need to bring a solar shower?

From personal experience, I will tout the amazing benefits of professionally installed solar hot water heaters in New Mexico. My disclaimer is that I'm not the professional that performed the installation and two more caveats; it was grid tied and expensive. This system only kicks in extra heat via electricity for cloudy days (i.e. when it's snowing and cold). Connected to roof mounted black sun soaking solar panels, the water was scalding hot on sunny days and never resorted to electricity, particularly during the height of summer. These systems require significant more investment than a standard water heater, but they are truly fantastic at providing copious amounts of soothing hot water using green energy. However, if you're living in a tiny house, this particular solar hot water heater was a beast and took up a lot of indoor space.

After you're freshly bathed, its time to sort out where that used tub/shower water goes. Incorporating a graywater system into your off-grid high desert life requires planning. Most often the pump used to filter the graywater out of the house needs electricity (unless it is gravity fed). Energetic people can happily bale buckets of water to the garden. The water you use washing dishes, doing laundry and bathing will require filtration as the water cannot sit stagnant in a holding tank. Being sanitary is essential so you'll probably want to use a professional gray water system rather than just funneling a PVC pipe into your backyard. Employ composting toilet philosophy and forget all about blackwater or the debate on how to use graywater to flush your commode.

I suppose on some level we could all follow in the footsteps of chickens and revel in dust baths. In the process gallons of water could be conserved. George Carlin was always a proponent of how much stronger our immune systems were prior to the invention of anti-bacterial soap. Now society is obsessed with scented body products, but we want them to be natural, not derivatives of a strawberry flavor manufactured in Hoboken, New Jersey. Purists can continue rubbing their armpits with deodorant crystals while pulling the psychic Uri Geller technique. Simply command the crystal to "work." Okay, I'm done damning deodorant crystals. Practically everyone within a hundred miles of Santa Fe or Taos has one, even me.

TALKIN' 'BOUT MY GENERATOR

Generators are the loudest word in off-grid living depending on your level of hardiness and your willingness to consume fossil fuels. Living off-grid during the winter is when you may have a strong desire to revel in back up power. Many generators on the market are sold for intermittent residential usage, a temporary back up during a grid power outage. This means you'll probably void your warranty when you run the crap out of it during January. You'll need to invest in a generator that can take heavy usage and has a decibel level that doesn't blast out the whole reason you moved to a remote area in the first place: solitude.

Military generators are the size of small cargo contain-

Utilities Nearby

ers. These are best sited far away from your sleeping quarters where you'll sleep in a tent with a built in iPad holder. In between the full on military base generator and the mini weekender/tailgate party battery powered model, you can strike a balance with a reliable Honda generator. It won't be fun and you'll be cheating your way through off-grid life, but it's only for a few months of the year.

Expect to shell out a couple grand for your back up generator. If you really want everything in life (and who doesn't), a generator is going to bridge the path of all your desires. Hug your giant propane tank for being there when you couldn't function during a lapse in solar power. Be happy propane is cheaper than gasoline and easier to store long term. Lower your electricity needs or go full tilt on a meaty generator worthy of American energy sucking consumption. For household emergency back up, you might get by with a 5000 KW generator. You'll be able to keep your freezer running and turn on a light bulb. Anything more than this basic minimalism means it's time to upgrade your generator KW. Let it rip and you'll be able to run one of those inflatable bouncy castles while running power tools, a hot plate and a hair dryer.

A WORD ON THAT QUAINT COTTAGE IN THE WOODS

Conspiracies about perfect people living in the woods often start on house forums. It begins after some independent filmmaker exuberantly runs off to create a short film about a couple living lightly on the land. Somehow the filmmaker has graciously been given what was formerly secret access to an idyllic lifestyle. Everything is just a little too quaint, from the covered porch to the blazing fireplace to the one saucepan stuffed with Brussels sprouts.

The short film goes on displaying a collection of dust

free hardback books and an oversized dictionary. One spouse has opted to forgo appearing in the film at all and thus is only referenced as a magical, enlightened being. During the several years of cabin living years, one spouse writes a single essay on living in the perfect cottage and then moves effortlessly into a career as an inspirational speaker. The filmmaker is told that every night incredible life changing conversations develop as the couple sit knee to knee in front of their fireplace.

 Like rabid javelina, what viewers initially perceived with curiosity and a touch of envy is quickly doused in a flammable liquid. Casual questions are then followed up with empirical research on Google. This leads to a house forum thread that is active for several years with hundreds of viewers wondering just what is the back story of the precious cottage goers. People get suspicious when Google reveals very little information and in frustration, note that there is more information about their own pathetic lives online than the quaint couple featured in the film.

 Initial comments remark about how the woman's clothes are too clean and how she appears freshly bathed. Someone else seconds the theory that there's no place to store food and there never was a mention of a garden. Someone else wonders if there's a storage shed that wasn't featured in the film. Finally an ex-girlfriend stumbles into the forum under the alias "Cucumber Sandwich" and sets things straight.

 I found myself captivated and then annoyed by these escapades into picturesque lives. That evening I read many comments and laughed harder than I had in a long time. I loved that other married couples, albeit happily, couldn't imagine sitting knee to knee with their spouse having deep, meaningful conversations every night. I was glad that not everyone else wanted to share a saucepan of Brussels sprouts with their lover in the name of living a green, quiet writer's life.

It reminded me of how burned out I am on every other person out there who finally figures it out then goes on to teach others about how they figured it out. Of course, this is all available in an online e-course for a small fee. This book in your hands ponders how I have and haven't figured it all out and I'm not yet selling an e-course. Stay tuned for my sequel and remember that when living situations appear perfect, there is some under current to which the viewer or reader is unaware.

It brings up how people watching tiny house videos write miffed comments when that Australian interviewer gets the effervescent story on another attractive couple who built a small house on their parents' land. Things like this drive people mad. I'm not here to sink dreams, I'm here to consider the pitfalls, cut through quaint pictures, over come it and live a decent enough life as a fallible human being.

READERS' COMMENTS

Haha, good one. Oh my god that's funny. They are abominations. You forgot to include that line. Well you survived anyway. How much did they charge you?

-Jeremy

Sounds like a total nightmare! BTW, I am in Taos County. I posted a link to your Craigslist ad on the Greater World Community Facebook page. Anyway, I wish you peace and much happiness from here on out.

Best, J.

Hi and thanks so much for answering my email and explaining a little more about off the grid experiences. My friend assures me he already has all the information on how to go about building his house and having the most efficient sources that we will need without having actual electricity. I am still a little skeptical as I never really had to rough it in my life, although I did have an unheated upstairs bedroom when I was growing up. So guess it's basically a decision I have to make, and trust it won't be as bad as I think. ugh! Lol. Thanks again.

-Jan

Question…read your ad. We are looking at properties for sale in Cerrillos, how bad is the internet when it is working? We will be "on grid", but I don't understand how the internet works, try as I might. Thanks so much, I was at least able to look up the La Canada site and get a better idea of how it all works. I understand the water is sketchy, we have

Utilities Nearby

a water test going now for a property we were interested in. Much appreciated!

-Anonymous

I had so much fun reading your "Solar Off Grid Savings" breakdown!
Turn your talent into a Blog on Off-Grid home/no home! You even covered the water.
I will be looking for that solar grid near Harry's.,,, and be thinking of you.

Cheers for deers!

Mikie

Jes, here is 10,000 watt system for $7K (http://www.ebay.com/itm/10-000-watt-solar-generator-HYBRID-16-Solar-Panel-System-ON-SALE-/261956195572?pt=LH_DefaultDomain_0&hash=item3cfdce54f4)

Still need batteries...BUT enough for most full on home usage.

M.

Subject: Sharpen Your Knife

Read http://santafe.craigslist.org/apa/...

You GOTTA make a public rebuttal to this! I think I am reading - No water without generator! OR NO WATER Too much dreamland to believe - CC me when you rip it online, please.

-M to J

Thanks for the heads up ... I did live in a solar housing outside of Madrid which I had to go around turning things off just to turn on other things ... it had a bathroom and good enough water from a little water tower. I am thinking of moving to Taos ... the Earthships sound kind of neat.

-Anonymous

Good Morning,
Thank you for your posting. I too love NM and am thinking of moving to a more "rustic" environment. Some of the cautions I know to stay away from, such as propane. Others I will definitely research more. Thanks again, the information was a real eye opener. Blessings to you and yours, and have a great day.

-Anonymous

I just wanted to thank you for that information, you put some time into it. Know a place with a great "view"? Cheers

-Anonymous

"It's like camping only you're paying $1000 a month" Bwhahahahahaha! So funny.

-Anonymous

You Rock! Thank you for your honest and informative post. Was curious and considering a few properties that state such things. I'm looking at list from out of state and don't want to waste any time with any such properties. Wishing you much happiness in your future endeavors, sounds like you were dealt a very bad hand. Appreciative for your insight.

-Michelle

Wait question? Why can't you drink the water in Cerrillos and Madrid? I knew the water table was messed up and thought that was why everyone had water holding- what's wrong with the water there.
I just bought land outside El Rito. Anything I'm supposed to know? I'll pay you to tell me. It has the Valecitos river on it and lots of grass. You guys can come up and camp for free if you want.

-Anonymous

Just wanted to say thank you, you are appreciated. With rents OUT of control every bit of information is important for the renter.

-Anonymous
Great info... Thanks for taking the time to be so thorough...

-Anonymous

I found your post to be very informative and helpful. I am curious what your thoughts are on properties listed for sale such as this one:

https://santafe.craigslist.org/...

It seems like a failed off-grid dream. I am now curious if the home will even stay warm with just a wood stove.

-Nicole

LOL, funny post. Thanks for the laugh!

-Anonymous

Hello, I'm interested in your off-grid house.

-Anonymous

WHAT'S HAWAII GOT TO DO WITH IT?

"Imagine no utility bills."
-New Mexico off the grid real estate listing

"The only utility renter pays is propane."
-Craigslist ad

Waiting in line at the grocery store, I glance at the magazines to get a grasp of popular culture. Every cover article these days mentions something about living "with intention." I couldn't help noticing how unrelated magazines paralleled each other: "Child Rearing with Intention" was just to the right of another magazine talking about, "Gardening with Intention." I'm unclear how generations of humanity managed these activities before intention came on the scene. Previously, we must have thoughtlessly reared children, tossed seeds in the dirt and drank lattes out of paper cups while stuck in traffic.

In the same way that foodie people post photographs of the meal they are currently eating, it seems nearly every magazine has a home section. Sometimes it might genuinely be an in house written article, but more typically the page is mashed into a paid advertisement section disguised as an article entitled "Interior Designs." If you look carefully, you'll find another ad of the same company or firm you coincidentally are reading an article about.

I was initially captivated by a full-page spread featuring a small beautiful home with a wall of sliding glass doors to bring the outside in. It was a humble 1000 square feet. The simple architecture suited me perfectly. Set into some southern "California Cowboy Country" I didn't know existed, "Just one hour from Los Angeles," the home was described verbatim as "Almost off the grid." That's like being almost, or somewhat pregnant. You're either on grid or you're not. Immediate stumbling followed with the laughable quote of the architect homeowner: "The only thing we're still tied into is power." Shame on you, *Cowboys and Indians Magazine.*

Let's define what "power" extends to when living almost off the grid. To southern Californians, does this simply mean that you installed a thousand dollar composting toilet? Power is everything to run the following all at once or in any fraction: Power is iPad charging for a family of four, heat your swimming pool, microwave popcorn, toast a bagel, boil water in an electric kettle, flip on a space heater, watch television, run a half dozen loads of laundry, use a trash compactor in the kitchen, run half the items sold on QVC and flip on a row of eight bathroom light bulbs, even when it's cloudy.

Granted, in the foothills of southern California, you won't need to blast a woodstove or radiant heat to keep warm. Avoiding a bone chilling cold winter alleviates a massive strain on the concept of *almost* off-grid. "Tied into power," means these Californians are feigning their way toward green earth mama's approval.

Compared with lifestyle alternatives such as van life, airport life or hotel life, a 1000 square foot home in a park like setting sounds rather luxurious. This perfect house, almost off-grid, was also described as "virtually maintenance free." Okay, vaulted metal roof. Great. Newer construction theoretically implies maintenance free for a solid decade, yet no house is maintenance free. In this delightful home example, it is still tied into grid power thus negating the need for batteries, inverters and solar photovoltaic systems. In magazines it's not just freshly made up models that get airbrushed. Lifestyles and cute little houses on glossy paper are there to make you envious, bitter and inferior. This is why I like reading tragic memoirs that cut to the chase.

* * *

Hawaii, as many might guess, uses less electricity than any other state in the union. Residents in Aloha land also pay more per kWh than any other state (still the cost is significantly less than an off-grid kWh). Although the rest of the United State is not Polynesian paradise, I like to use Hawaii as a benchmark for what to expect when going off-grid. Since the United States is one of the energy junkies of the world it seems most fitting to compare off-grid aspirations to the gentler Hawaiian standard, which more accurately equates with the rest of the modern world's energy usage.

Have a gander at the light pollution map of the world depicting satellite images of brightly lit urban centers. Notice the vast black swatch between Montana and New Mexico. Here in sparsely populated New Mexico, our black skies still boast starry nights. Even in Albuquerque, visitors from sprawling metropolitan areas marvel about how the sky is actually dark. Still, it's nice to turn on the occasional lamp in the evening. Numerous New Mexico properties make one notation, "High tech solar system in place." What exactly does that mean for a New Mexico off-grid property?

From my numerous readings, let's first break down electricity usage in Hawaii:

18 kWh = Daily average
544 kWh = Monthly average
6528 kWh = Annual average
$0.33 = The average cost per kWh in Hawaii.

Here is a comparison to New Mexico's annual average household electricity consumption:

21 kWh = Daily average
655 kWh = Monthly average
11,052 kWh = Annual average
$0.13 = The average cost per kWh in New Mexico.

As an example, we can compare a robust 10,000 kilo-watt photovoltaic solar array and it's estimated output based on New Mexico sun exposure. This estimate is in conjunction with a well cared for battery bank operating at full sun everyday for optimal performance. This is the maximum amount of electricity you could theoretically generate if everyday for one year was sunny and every month had the daylight hours of summer light.

10,000 watts x 5.5 (sun hours) = 55,000 watts
− 20% loss of 11,000 watts / by 1000 =

44 kWh = Daily
1320 kWh = Monthly
15,840 = Annually

In the above equation your available energy equates with Louisiana, the state that uses the most electricity in the United States according to national energy statistics. Remember, this estimate applies if everyday in New Mexico for 365 days is sunny based on 5.5 daily hours of full sun. Please note that this is a general rough estimate and like weight loss programs, other factors will influence the precise amount of electricity available for your system. Mother nature has variables.

Again, there is nothing wrong with adapting to seasonal changes, it's how our ancestors lived. Sometimes rather than complaining it's better to simply be prepared. That way you aren't surprised when old man winter blows onto your mesa. In the winter, to be prudent, you might cut the above perky estimate of your 10K system by 50% or possibly a little more:

$$22 \text{ kWh} = \text{Daily}$$
$$660 \text{ kWh} = \text{Monthly}$$
$$7920 \text{ kWh} = \text{Annually}$$

Clearly, with a 10K watt solar array, you're sporting a comfortable off-grid life without foregoing luxury comforts. At the time of this writing, such a system will cost over $20,000.

If you splurge on the ultra efficient lithium deep cycle batteries, over lead acid, add a few more thousand. Lithium batteries are more robust than the less expensive lead acid batteries. However, lithium batteries are hulks and you won't single handedly unload these hefty beasts from the back of your pick up truck. They weigh a lot more than golf cart batteries, but you'll need fewer lithium batteries and they do have a longer life span.

Lithium batteries are also better adapted to more depth of discharge (DOD) than the lead acid variety. In the long run, you'll save money by investing in lithium batteries, unless you rent out your off-grid home to people who don't know what they are doing, because it's frequently assumed that off-grid living is virtually maintenance free.

Let's look at a real life example of a "Magical Off the Grid Retreat" available in northern New Mexico. This was a reply I received for a rental home on Craigslist. The system was installed "a few years ago." The house has:

> 4 x 180 Watt Solar Panels with
> 8 lead acid deep cycle batteries

Convert the maximum kWh available with this system. We will multiply by 5.5, the number of peak daylight hours available for New Mexico (or Zone 2 according to most solar company maps).

To the solar panel manufacturer, "peak hours" translates to High-Noon-Sun-Tanning-in-a-Chaise-Lounge-Big-Sunglasses-Bikini-Wearing-Hot-Sun. The Zone's number of hours (in this case 5.5) relates to the STC (Standard Testing Conditions) which means it's high noon sun all the time in the optimal world of testing solar panel out put. It's similar to car testing for gas mileage. Ideal conditions for any aspect of life are typically fleeting. I say this not as a pessimist, but as a prepper.

Ideal conditions also means that during those blazing sunny hours of testing, that not one fluffy cloud or enticing mesa shadow mitigated your maximum wattage output. Note that the 5.5 peak sun hours never include morning daylight hours nor the last hours of daylight leading to "The park closes at sunset."

> 4 solar panels x 180 Watts x 5.5 = 3960 watts.

Utilities Nearby

Multiply by 80% to account for an average of 20% general energy inefficiency in any system. This is the energy lost to produce energy. Solve this problem and you'll rule the world. It's sort of a Catch 22 as your system (inverter) converts battery energy from DC (Direct Current) to AC (Alternating Current).

Maximum watts available after accounting for 20% loss = 3168 Watts. Divide 1000 watts because 1 kWh = 1000 Watts. In this real life example, you are living on 17.47% of the energy consumed by the average resident in Hawaii. Granted, in New Mexico, you won't be blasting an air-conditioner as you might in your Waikiki condo.

Total maximum daily kWh for the Magical Off Grid Retreat under optimal sunny conditions:

>3.168 kWh = Daily
>95 kWh = Monthly
>1140 kWh = Annually

This calculation will be a good rough estimate of your available power during the summer months. During the winter, it will be less. On this particular system, you're severely curtailing your electricity usage. This set up is suitable for the bare bones individual (not the typical couple or family).

Hats off to the people who can really ace this lifestyle. Four solar panels are for someone who mostly lives naked in the woods and occasionally plugs in an iPad so they can rant at me on Craigslist (pardon my twisted humor).

I know I was born after the light bulb was invented. For millennia, previous civilizations got by without electricity except on those History Channel documentaries about aliens and the lost technologies of Mesopotamia, the Egyptians and the Aztecs. These people invented spark plugs before Steve Jobs' Paleolithic ancestors were born.

Some off-grid rhetoric touts a blind campaign, "Imagine no utility bills." Just ignore the fact that you spent a couple thousand on batteries, solar panels, an inverter and a control panel. The tradeoff in going 100% off-grid is investing in the next twenty years of your electricity usage upfront. Your cost per kWh is more off-grid and you'll have less to use than savoring the convenience of the electric company, but you will be master of your destiny. Budget to replace your bank of batteries during the next decade and maybe your electricity bill isn't so bad.

In your off-grid home, minus a lot of guests who accidentally leave the lights on, and being someone that doesn't watch T.V. or require internet to work from home, you can forge a doable life on a 5000 watt system. Some weeks during the winter won't be great and you might take your laundry to town, but it's a small price to pay for "tranquility." Then again you're now paying to do laundry, which is still technically a utility bill of sorts.

The Earthship folks wonder how I can be so unimaginative and skeptical. Probably because their website speaks much about "systems" without ever mentioning kWh (at least last I checked). Yes, I've closed my eyes and practiced the fine art of visualizing my dreams, but that's not teaching me how to run numbers or make sales. Basic math skills are required if you want more in your off-grid life than sponge baths. Remember, we are planning to live off-grid for the rest of our lives and there's no going back! At least not without the on grid hecklers and our tail between our legs shaming us with, "I told you so."

UTILITIES NEARBY

You want amenities like electricity, even if you're ready to embrace a composting commode or that dreamy outhouse. Now you're on Google wondering how many appliances you can live without while you live the dream. My bare bones off-grid life calculation involves a single household appliance, a half-liter electric Bodum kettle, which uses 700 Watts to boil a .05 liter of water. It's 120 Volts/60 hz. This humble little kettle is a great example because it's a small heat source household appliance that is incredibly functional.

Rather than focusing on the bells and whistles of a 10K watt or even 5K watt solar array, we will build from pure minimalism using this electric kettle as my one essential home appliance for off-grid living. I'm not saying you need an electric kettle, it's just an example. That 05. liter of hot water makes coffee, tea, and a hot wash cloth to clean one's face a reality. It also prepares instant dehydrated black bean soup and offers the enjoyment of hot ramen noodles whilst writing your novel. All of this is possible without starting a fire or using propane when you have enough power for a 700 watt kettle.

For those that want to share their 0.5 liter of water with a significant other I'll allot daily use of this appliance to 1 hour per day. The kettle takes a little less than 5 minutes to boil. That means I can boil 0.5 hot water 12 times using my kettle for exactly 1 hour in a 24 hour period. This hot water allocates: Coffee for two in the morning, soup for two in the afternoon, tea for two in the evening, two hot water bottles, a warm up for two and hot sponge baths for two.

My interest in the small kettle stems from a desire to go glamping. It's for considering those times when wind and rain is blowing, making a campfire difficult or for the times when it's late at night and I want a hot tea while camping in my 4Runner. It's for those times where I might not have a tipi and one of those micro heater stoves, but I have a solar panel and a deep cycle battery set up like all the other YouTube wilderness goers.

The 700 Watt 120 Volt AC kettle electricity usage breaks down like this for one year:

700 watts x 1 hour use per day = 700 watts / 1000 = 0.70

kWh per day
2 kWh = per month
252 kWh = per year

I need to generate at least 1 kWh per day to use my kettle. Theoretically, I'm still camping in New Mexico so in I need a minimum of 2 x 100 Watt 12V portable flexible solar panels suitable for RV's x 5.5 hours of sun per day. On sunny days, I could generate about 0.88 kWh per day with this set up and run the kettle for an hour per day. However, it is important to consider that as I'm typing this sentence it's a cold and cloudy day in New Mexico. Therefore, I'll have to cut back on my kettle usage on such days. If you don't want to reach for your calculator, the amps to run this kettle are figured like this:

700 Watts ÷ 120 Volts AC = 5.83 Amps

The amperage tells me what I will need in a battery bank so I can store my solar power for my late night kettle power usage. A fully charged basic golf cart battery operating at maximum capacity breaks down like this:

35Ah x 12V = 420 Wh or 0.42 kWh

Of course, it's a bad idea to discharge a golf cart battery (or any deep cycle battery) completely and in the above example I'd be squeezing the life out of this battery making

Utilities Nearby

it obsolete in no time. If I were judicious, a 50% discharge would produce 0.21 kWh per day. I can consider cutting the number of times I boil water to 6 x per day instead of 12 meaning my kettle uses 0.35 kWh per day. Clearly, I'm not living the high life, nor running my kettle on a single golf cart battery. Too bad because a golf cart battery only weighs about 16 lbs, costs under $100 and would easily work into car camping. Let's say I go with a 100Ah 12V deep cycle battery.

$$100 \text{ Ah} \times 12\text{V} = 1200 \text{ Wh} / 1000 = 1.2 \text{ kWh}$$

In this instance, I'm making my kWh quota, but my battery now weighs over 60 lbs and it's the size of a medium cooler. Taking a battery like this camping begs the question of whether I even qualify as a stealth camper or if I'm headed toward honker RV life just so I can power my electric kettle. Such a battery costs under $200 and it will last for a few years (about 2-5) depending on my level of conscious living vs. neglect.

Adding a charge controller will mitigate the volatile shifts in mother nature's rays thus regulating current recharge. I err on the side of minimal battery cycles when estimating the lifetime of the battery because people aren't perfect. I'm essentially combining incompatible elements: nature and comfort.

Remember that just because you slapped a solar panel on your retro Westfalia VW bus, if it is lying flat, or not positioned to take full advantage of solar rays, you will have slower recharging times. It is no different than sitting all day by a pool and repositioning your chaise lounge for optimal tan/sunburn.

I once remember staring at the extra 12V plug in the back of my Honda Element and wishing that I could run my Bodum kettle on a car camping trip. This isn't a rehashing of my earlier commenting on cappuccino machines, it was merely an innocent example of one convenient household appliance. I really do love the outdoors and I really do love hot coffee and tea. Combining these elements is precisely what "glamping" is all about. I do own an ultra-light backpacker propane stove so this theorizing over car camping with my electric kettle is over.

ON THE GRID SOLAR POWER TIE IN

There's another category in the solar power world for those enjoying on the grid lives in neighborhoods with street lights and sidewalks. They are the ones relishing on grid power plus a roof covered in solar panels. This supplemental energy makes sense particularly because excess power is sold back to the power company. It works because the homeowner does not have to store energy for later use. Essentially, the on grid homeowner with solar panels, has a meter that can run backwards. They save money when the sun is out, but if cloudy days loom, there is no sacrifice in available power because they can tap Uncle Grid Power.

What is intriguing to me is that while on grid homeowners utilize solar, their photovoltaic systems often outpace the capabilities of many off the grid properties of northern New Mexico. It seems that typically on grid supplemental folks install at least 5000 capable watts of solar panels on their roofs, compared to the hard core energy conserving, or paltry solar systems of some off the grid folks.

Solar is not a one size fits all enterprise, but a lot of us ask questions that seem logical enough. After doing away with all the solar formulas everyone winds up on Quora or

Utilities Nearby

Reddit and wants to know, "Yeah, but what does it actually take to be comfortable off the grid?"

We want that temperature range of 72 degrees Fahrenheit that most humans thrive at. Everyone eventually is faced with the same questions like, "How much power can I store, at what cost and for how long?" That's the biggest kicker in everything we do since most of our lives are reliant on rechargeable batteries. Nature and nurture applies to battery care too as I am reminded of my personal experience living off-grid in the worst conditions possible, including tired, neglected, freezing batteries.

One of the inefficiencies in deep cycle batteries is the fact that the supply to them is perpetually inconsistent. This means batteries can wear out more quickly because not everyday has the exact same blazing sunny conditions (or the same amount of wind). Your energy usage will also be variable unless you are an extreme obsessive compulsive and those you live with also exhibit extreme obsessive compulsive behavior. Such folks will climb out of bed at the exact minute as the day previously and everyday after. Because the movie *Groundhog Day* is a figment of urban legends, no one except Bill Murray will ever have such an experience except possibly the people living in a monastery and those people don't care if they have an electric kettle.

We can all bask in sunny New Mexico knowing that even living a sinful life on the grid, we're using approximately 24% less energy per month than the national average. Solar and energy technology will steadily improve as long as some epic asteroid doesn't collide with the earth. We can talk about the theoretical or the inevitable depending on your serotonin levels. No matter what, off-grid batteries currently still cost a couple thousand dollars.

Adapting to life on solar power (and other non-grid tied energy sources) is largely influenced by how you curtail your energy usage. It is not actually about flipping the bird at the utility company and buying a few solar panels. You can do it, but you will live with less electricity. Off set with gas or propane or forego certain appliances or conveniences.

If you wanted to emulate the on grid scenario of the average on grid New Mexican, this translates to approximately 24 x 250 Watt solar panels + 20% more to account for the pesky loss of energy it takes to make energy. You'll also plan for a 25% drop in available power that happens during those shorter winter days. Cloudy weather will affect you, but not in the Seasonally Affected Disorder kind of way.

Utilities Nearby

READERS' COMMENTS

I enjoy off grid living in any weather. Then again before moving to the city, I grew up on a farm that still used an outhouse. I wanted to thank you for your post and say that I agree with you 100%. What most people don't realize is the inflated rent for an unfinished structure is a rip off. This is typically city folk just looking to make a buck.

-Anonymous

Hi, I am curious about your article on off the grid...LOL. I never heard this term before, until recently, when a friend of mine says he has land in San Luis Valley, Colorado and isn't far from Taos, New Mexico. So he says he wants to build a house there to retire, he can have a well and septic put in but he told me electricity is pretty much non-existent and started talking about solar panels and propane generators. Are these functional and/or costly?

So you seem to be quite informed on all that, so before I agree to possibly move there and retire in this "off the grid" lifestyle, maybe you can educate me more on if these alternate electricity plans really work, and if the weather there really gets cold in the winter and basically I want to know if I will be freezing to death HAHA. And what advice on what is best to get when he builds this house to make it somewhat functional.

Sorry, but I am a woman and its hard for me to imagine living my days out in the wild, without some modern convenience. I must mention that I have sleep apnea and need a c-pap machine to breathe at night. So you can see my concern if I will be able to get some energy to power this. Decisions, decisions...being out in nature sounds so

tempting, but scary at the same time so any input you can give me, would be deeply appreciated.
Thanks so much.

-Jan

Thanks so much for answering my email and explaining a little more about off the grid experiences. My friend assures me he already has all the information on how to go about building his house and having the most efficient sources that we will need without having actual electricity. I am still a little skeptical as I never really had to rough it in my life, although I did have an unheated upstairs bedroom when I was growing up. So I guess it's basically a decision I have to make, and trust it won't be as bad as I think. Ugh! LOL… so thanks again.

-Jan

Thank you!! New to NM from East Coast… Great education, please put me on your mailing list
Best wishes, Jed

 I've also thought it interesting how, after the incredible amount of time, money, and effort it took someone to create an off grid home why they don't live there themselves. So now I know why. Thanks so much and keep posting.
-N

Hi,
I'm a solar tech, natural builder, permaculture designer, off-grid homesteader. I've lived with and without power, running water, heat, etc for many years. It's a lifestyle. I will say one pays one way or another to learn the ins and outs of the lifestyle. I see many interesting points in your posting. I see

Utilities Nearby

questionable decisions by both the renter and the owner. I made many myself. There's a cost to learning and experiencing.

I think the rental price should reflect the condition and circumstances. $700-$1200 sounds very high unless there are other attributes included such as waterfront, views, acreage, location, workshop space, etc. I don't agree with an owner who takes advantage of one renter after another each winter. That seems unethical unless things are clearly understood by all and the price reflects it.

One example I would point to is the batteries. I see both sides of the coin. If I was an owner I would hesitate to spend $2000-$4000 on new batteries for a renter. In the solar business we call them "starter batteries." They often get ruined by newbies especially if they did not have to pay for them, or for a new replacement battery bank. I would consider charging much less rent and either providing old batteries or ask the renter to bring batteries with them. Then there's liability. Is it wise to have a renter tinkering with a power plant? You posed many interesting questions. Off-grid opens up a can of worms for real estate rental.

Now I have two solar motor homes. A big one and a small one. And three storage trailers. As I was unsure of either owning or renting this is my stopgap measure. I put everything on wheels after several very trying experiences being fixed to the ground.

It would be nice to see something balanced in your posting. How nice it can be to live with the cycles of nature and the seasons. How much one can learn about the basics of comfort and self-reliance. What solutions did you craft? Did you build a decent woodstove? I've seen pictures of NM and drove through the mountains once. There's wood there.

Did you show much initiative? Why not get interested in the laws of thermodynamics and apply them?

The first reading was humorous but the second came to sound like a rant. Which is ok if it is stated as such. The old tensions between renters and owners is fertile ground for debate. My impression of the Santa Fe area was not favorable for me. I would enjoy reading the responses you received if you will share them with me. Thank you.

-Anonymous

I'm from Washington, but hanging in Florida for now. Getting ready to sell my short bus as I like to work on everything except what makes money LOL. Sometimes when I'm consulting or designing an energy system I joke asking if they have changed the diapers on their batteries today. In other words have they babied them, given them lots of attention, and cleaned up the caustic mess they cause. We call them "starter batteries." After ruining a battery bank and spending thousands to replace them, they take better care of the second set. How's your relationship with your batteries going LOL? Remove the rose tinted glasses at the power shed. It's numbers, logic, chemistry, laws of thermodynamics, potential energy, hardware, software, and some TLC to top it off. How many replies have you collected? Are you a social engineer? Cheers!

-Jeremy

Hi again from Jeremy, it's been a while. Boy howdy sounds like Santa Fe has lost much of its charm and is overpriced. Had not seen your rant in a while. I've lived off-grid for ages. Still living in one of my buses and sometimes freeze my butt. I can see maybe $300-400 per month and a discount in winter for the places you describe. They need to be cheap because it is like another job. One thing to consider is that twelve L16 batteries is about $4000. Twelve golf cart batteries is over $2000. I wouldn't leave those with a rental. It's a bad recipe. BYOB. Bring your own batteries LOL. That might be a good way to screen folks who really love and are devoted to off-grid living?

I'm a bit confused. A well-designed straw bale house with a good woodstove and dry wood should be cozy. A lot of cabins have the wrong type of stove for the type of construction. And patterns of use are important. Yes, newbie off-gridders often get into trouble.

Have you gotten to try a house, cabin, bus, anything with radiant floor heat? I built one and loved it. It can be efficient to heat the objects in the space via radiation than heat every air molecule and all the mass of a house. That's my two cents worth.

-Jeremy

Interesting article. Thanks for sharing. What inspired you to post this? My intentions are to move to the area in June and I am very interested in self-sustaining methods of living. I have been for thirty years. Seems I've been distracted by other things, until now. Haha. Hopefully I can find work there too.

-Anonymous

Hey there! I sure appreciate the dialogue! Sounds like there's the right way to be off-grid, and then there's the miserable way of doing it! I might tap your wisdom from time to time especially as I move closer. I left Oklahoma in April for east TX where my sister is preparing to move west of Saguache, CO where she and my Mom have recently purchased a "dude ranch" property. My Mom has extensive experience in this area. They are leaving Chama, to do so (my mom). After I get my sister moved up to CO I will be making my way to the northern NM region to work and explore for at least a while. Self-sustaining lifestyle has always been a curiosity and passion and I am particularly fascinated by wind and solar. Late night here. Thanks again. May your day be full of enough warmth and electricity!

-Ken

THE TAOS HIPPIE REBUTTAL

"Rented a yurt north of Taos. No running water, no indoor plumbing. Loved it. There you go. A happy experience."

-Craigslist reply

Over the course of my chronic re-posting on Craigslist, I received a few replies that did not commend the content of my educational and cathartic rant. By far, the number of replies I received revering my post exceeded the Negative Nancies. The enthusiasm and support of my post has been the crowning moment of my adult life. It was never my intent to dissuade all from living off the grid, but rather a commentary on how ludicrous it was to pay high rent for doing so just because it was Santa Fe.

My unsolicited experience seemed to resonate or I would never have achieved so much community, simply by posting on Craigslist. The truth is that even I have some hippie inclinations, so in naming this chapter, it is tongue in cheek. I get where the following people are coming from. Lawless paradise amongst the sage brush and no one bothering anyone else, all under the New Mexico sun is a common dream around here. I share that vision too, even amongst the naysayers.

Although, if the following people are already living a life of off-grid bliss, why are they perusing Santa Fe/Taos house rentals and thus encountering my post? I just didn't think average people wanted to pay high rent for such rustic living conditions. My rambling on the pit falls of off-grid living were nothing more than a cathartic form of compassion (and a vendetta against one measly landlord). Below are a few of my favorite replies.

READERS' COMMENTS

Actually I have lived off-grid in that location and it was doable and not expensive...I live in Florida now. I think I will write the truth about YOUR post and report you.

-Lia

Better call a wahhhmbulance, you sound really hurt.

-Thebes

You obviously have your head up your ass sir. Earthships are great and just because you chose to live in a crappy one doesn't mean you should project your garbage onto the world. You are the kind of pathetic imbecile that will help man take two steps back and zero forward. Good day.

Best regards,
M.

Rented a yurt north of Taos. No running water, no indoor plumbing. Loved it. There you go. A happy experience. Now why don't you take your know it all brand of negativity that can only come from one who has never lived off the grid or in the elements, plug in your baseboard heat, turn on your internet porn and have a great time. Leave the real living and real life experiences to those of us who are equipped to handle them, derive pleasure from them and watch HGTV or some other reality show.

-Anonymous

"Off-grid" is a misnomer. There are roads and cell service in most areas everywhere...thus there is really no such thing as "off-grid." I have lived for thirty years 6 miles southwest of the gorge bridge "off-grid" very comfortably and happily. I have rented homes as long and I am continually amazed at the ignorance of most people.

The biggest part of the stupidity is the lack of understanding energy in the form of heat and electricity. So fools are befuddled when their solar filled battery runs out. They simply can't do basic arithmetic and division. These same folks have no idea where electricity comes from (Fukushima or Four Corners power plant spewing mercury and other great stuff). Or how many forests are being decimated to build Uglyville in New Jersey or to heat homes? "Off-grid" living is an attempt, be it amateur, to simplify thus avoiding pollution, environmental degradation and excessive energy consumption. Go live in town.

-Stephen

LOL funny stuff all of these issues definitely have solutions but my thinking is if you can't figure it out go back to the grid. I love being off-grid sure it was rough at first especially with the propane cost but now I spend 40 bucks a month on propane thanks to good old wood. As for solar it has not let me down yet but anyone who doesn't have a backup generator has not thought about clouds or even hail. Not being able to think outside the grid is proof that people are forgetting their natural skill set. Soon people won't know how to cook or clean or start a fire. Everyone wants to go off-grid and grow pot and chill out...LOL not gonna happen you have to get up and do stuff like wipe the snow off of your panels at the crack of dawn so you can watch the news. Or maybe the wild horses are kicking the mirrors off of your truck so you go chase 'em off, etc. You never know what to expect when everything relies on you not the energy company or the county, just you. There is a way to make it work but you need to be realistic if you want to rent or rent out. You can't charge grid prices when you can't offer it's benefits. $100 bucks a month in my eyes is top dollar I'd never expect to pay or collect a penny more for a raw land rental. Hell, you can buy some plots for a little more than $100 month.

-Anonymous

Dude. You really need to get over yourself. I have lived off the grid in Northern NM. I lived in a Strawbale house in Colorado when it was -30 degrees, and I was COMPLETELY WARM!!!! Strawbale houses are the warmest houses you can get! Your walls are a foot thick for crying out loud! I have never used propane for off the grid because it is not off the grid. A woodstove is enough to heat a passive solar or strawbale house. And why is it so important to have a fridge in the winter? Just put a giant freezer or fridge outside and DONT plug it in! Your food will stay cold. It's winter. The real key is to be a vegetarian and only have dehydrated foods like beans and rice that don't go bad. Grow vegetables in the spring and summer. Most gourds will last a year before they go bad. Many root vegetables will last the winter. The rest can be dehydrated easily without electricity. It's called a desert. And what is so important about having electricity? We all benefit from not having EMFs (electro magnetic fields) around us. If you need to

Utilities Nearby

see at night, get some solar lamps from the Dollar Tree for a dollar! If you need internet, go to the library. If you need T.V., something serious is wrong with you and why are you even talking about off the grid anyway? In this day and age, especially now that we live in a very scary climate for the ecology of our country and the whole earth thanks to the evil Satanists who have taken over our country, we need to encourage off the grid living now more than ever! Seriously, everyone knows off the grid living is roughing it. I know of hundreds living off the grid in Tres Piedras alone, and they survive the winter just fine. Just because you are too pussy to take one for the team doesn't mean you should be speaking out against those who care more about the environment than they do their own creature comforts. I think it's time to take your unnecessary rant off of Craigslist.

-Anonymous

Loved your article, built my Adobe hacienda 80 acres off-grid 2 story, quite a learning curve, it truly is not for everyone, diesel generator backup & I have seen 10' degrees below for ten days. Plenty of truth in your words but I'd rather be up here than down there. Been here since 1999. I am a horse person & I love the solitude, thanks for your article. Loved it!

-Randy

Good Morning: This post made me laugh. I lived off the grid in California, ten miles up a rough dirt road, in a yurt. It was one of those "spiritual community" situations. Everything you wrote is TRUE. LOL Thank you for trying to spare the utopia seekers a bit of misery. Have a great day.

-Patricia

I found your post to be filled with useful information. Especially for people who are for the first time potentially considering living "off-grid" and the points you make about propane and PV systems are right on. I am curious if you can share the Bewitched by Earthships story? Thanks.

-Jacob

I must say that your diatribe (no offense) was very informative and truly accurate. I have a '57 Airstream trailer and got an 80w solar panel and a big battery. It was educational. I learned one thing- well more than one thing- but in fact deep cycle batteries aren't supposed to be drawn down lower than 50% or they are damaged, and cold temps- also bad. Hot temps also bad. So off the grid- yeahh. Monastery- and you are so correct about snow on the panels. Anyway- I hope lots of folks read that. Sounds like a rough learning curve for you. I've been thinking about moving to northern New Mexico, but yeahh 7000 feet is up there, even if it doesn't snow.

Thank God for LED light bulbs though, right?

-Karl

Thanks for swift response. I'm sorry to hear you are turned off to off-grid living now. I believe it can be done relatively comfortably depending on needs, budget, skills, and expectations. It can cramp ones style for some people and enhances it for others. As I mentioned there's a cost for the desire. I spent countless days, months, and years learning systems at the expense of family, social, and career trade offs. Experiments with energy cost thousands and are long-term investments. I had to walk away from a bunch of unfinished projects. The place you rented sounds "sub standard." You could likely have taken your landlord to court and won a judgment.

My experience is that solar is amazing but insufficient for most people and situations. "Cogeneration" of solar with microhydro, or wind (high maintenance however) is much improved. A generator at the very least is usually needed except by expert off-grid users. Efficiency is the key. Batteries are a slippery slope. A watchful eye on every watt of power gains longevity but this is difficult when more than one person uses the system. Added adults or children leaving things on or using inefficient loads and it's a recipe for low voltage alarms, brown outs, potential blackouts, and possible discord and disharmony. Many people are not interested enough to learn how to care and feed their batteries. Perhaps if they had to pay for batteries…however…

I have sometimes used the analogy of batteries as babies. "Have you cared and fed your batteries?" "Have you changed their diapers." The people who look at me like I'm crazy probably never go on to owning or caring for an off-grid system.

I built a propane boiler radiant floor heating system that was pretty efficient. So I would not write off propane entirely. It used about 350 gal per winter here in mild Pacific northwest, but for a big house. We had a woodstove back up too. It got to 18 degrees. Brrrr....9 degrees, that's bone chilling.

I'm rather surprised how little folks do to enhance their comfort and finances in this regard. A friend lived in a leaky old farmhouse for 16 years and endured very inefficient stove and furnace. If they had simply redesigned and remodeled immediately they would have saved a small fortune let alone all the feeding of the stove. They even had the money to do it. This is partly due to the short sighted and short-term focus of this society. But I have lost my shirts several times by investing time, effort, and money into long-term goals. Now my goals have wheels as my budget does not allow for land and taxes currently. I'm currently building one of the only bus conversions with radiant floor heat.

I know a guy and daughter who don't turn heat on at all in Vancouver, WA. The house is 40-50 degrees in winter. 60 degrees on a rare sunny day. However he made a big foil backed foam insulation box over each bed for the winter. They are cozy at night with body heat. LOL.

Well, enjoyed chatting with you. If you feel like sharing some responses, that's wonderful. Oh, the suburban sprawl and traffic we saw developing around Santa Fe and Albuquerque was a turn off to us. We were there in the 60's and 70's.

Best wishes,
Jeremy

Hello, Interesting take on the New Mexico ren al scene. I'm thinking of what I have been doing in Minnesota for the past twenty years, and the one primary agreeable part is the problem to produce heat via solar. The small Sundanzer fridge at the farm and house in the city and the freezer in another house are great and just sip juice ....so they really don't tax the system. The real issue we have is to lug in water...because we are primarily lazy about filtering... and trips back into town is not that much of an inconvenience.

I have had 3-5 extended days with out much power production...for the photovoltaic, and have still been able to run the Sundanzer refrigerator ....lighting at night and possibly DVD player/LED T.V. For the system what we have

Utilities Nearby

is pared down to be pretty minimal: 150 watts of panels (vintage 1975) with only 2 six volt batteries to run the works. As long as we are mindful about the morning starting voltage (prior to the sun starting the charging cycle) we can assess the ongoing health of the batteries and how much we could/would test the loads we draw later in the day. Currently with the living space within the shed at the farm I only have two full hour of good charging time near noon. Otherwise, there are trees that deny the charging on the west side of noon. It has not been a problem and I have not had to aggressively think about clearing more sun space for charging ...because we are not taxing the batteries as it is currently working.

I think the real big issue for folks who would come out to visit and to live/work/ play and deal with limitations is the outhouse, a way to clean up (bathing) and potable water. Since this is really more of a temporary situation where we are coming out for 2 to 5 days max at a time, we can bring the food/water to meet our needs.

The thing that I am really pleased with, with the new outlook for solar is the readily available tools that can be charged off an AC inverter system. So far....most everything with the normal running of the solar system is simply tapping into the charged 12 volt batteries (in series) with a small 160 watt inverter that goes for $20 bucks.

Not much of an outlay for money and a lot of return to have basic electrical needs for comfort. I do believe we as a culture need more of these experiences to see how easy it is to meet our electrical needs and how much we do not need to be tapped in to the grid to make for a more modern lifestyle.

-B. V of Minneapolis

Don't be so down. I built my adobe, straw bale off-grid house at 8000 ft and it's the toastiest, nicest place on earth. Pipes don't freeze, never run out of power. And yes the old Pavoni espresso machine works just fine on my little 12 V system with 6 (2V) batteries! It is possible. It just takes a lot of planning.

-Fiona

THE GAUNT VEGAN: EATING OFF-GRID

"Just put a giant freezer or fridge outside and don't plug it in!"

-Craigslist reader

Diet is intrinsically tied to our homes and it goes hand in hand in the off grid world. I'm not a health coach, a dietician, nor one of the creators of the original food pyramid. Conspiracies about the food and agriculture associations influencing the iconic food pyramid are a story for another time. Next to choosing a home and spouse, as long as one is not literally starving, diet is a personal health and cultural choice. From peanut butter and florescent orange cheese crackers to the South Beach Diet, there are many options including: Paleo eater, vegetarian, vegan, raw vegan, "mostly vegan," pescatarian, flexitarian, locavore, freegan, and fruitarian to name a few.

I spent several years as a vegetarian until the day I desperately cracked open a can of tuna fish saying, "I'm so sorry little fish." Then I proceeded to open the packet of relish and crackers. Being the kind of person that loses weight just sitting in an armchair makes it difficult for me to adapt to my friend's virtually fat free diet, the friend who always feeds me shrimp and udon noodles. I stand in awe of people that don't get hypoglycemic and who enjoy long runs at 5:00 in the morning. These folks must have bionic bodies and somehow a few of them thrive on a vegan diet. I can't possibly chop firewood off the grid and be vegan.

I've been frustrated yet fascinated by the vegan concept for a long time, hence naming this chapter, "The Gaunt Vegan". I apologize in advance to those that quietly eat vegan without wearing a t-shirt about it. On my last visit to a juice bar, I felt like a Neanderthal. The girl in line behind me was wearing a t-shirt that read *Love Animals Don't Eat Them*. It reminded me of the time I finally got an interview with a non-profit that told me I would have to be vegan in their office and if I ate cheese, I better leave it in my car.

It's unfortunate that some vegans put a bad name on all vegans by preaching the hell out of the lifestyle. It was just the other day when a friend met me in Santa Fe at the French pastry restaurant even though she has celiac disease. It was clear to me that during weekend brunch, the vegan deli next door was doing significantly less business than the place selling buttery croissants and quiche.

The irony is that the vegan place is leasing out a portion of the building to the croissant people. Maybe it's not worth a dissertation in mentioning, but congruency and integrity eventually translates to, "We're all doing the best we can even if it's not perfect, which is better than not trying at all."

Since the dawn of civilization, what we eat and it's effects on our world, morality, health and body will continue to be dissected at length. All of us can learn to adapt to others perspectives, but then the whole point of living off-grid is to live freely by one's personal rhetoric. Perhaps it's okay that you still eat green chile cheeseburgers and your friend eats Benevolent Bacon. Many meat eaters hail the Paleo diet as the healthiest path of humanity's continuation based on a caveman diet. Michael Pollan, author of Omnivore's Dilemma, still eats meat occasionally as proclaimed on his website. Although Pollan articulates his position in a matter of fact manner, some people are still bothered. Equally well-known journalist Lisa Ling still eats meat even after a visit to a slaughterhouse and receiving expert guidance on vegan grocery shopping.

People squawk about being sustainable regardless of their preferred eating habits. For some, sustainable means legumes and bottles of Beano like in the cabinets of the Upaya Zen Center, or so I was told. The plant based protein tribe touts that bloating is just a reflection of a body detoxifying itself. Coming off a diet rife with breakfast burritos and tamales, the toxic body slowly learns to regale the mighty lentil.

I too can cook dhal and once tried to emulate a vegan by cooking carrots and coconut milk. Strict plant-based eaters tell me if I could just stick with the lentils program, the planet will love me better. Some plant-based eaters are okay with dining beside a carnivore. Then there are nearly militant vegans who won't eat at the same table while someone else eats an animal based product. Such divergent ideologies touch on the concept I mentioned earlier about living in a "like minded community."

My complaining about not having enough power to run a small refrigerator off the grid infuriated at least one Craigslist reader. The gist being, "If you don't eat meat, you don't need a fridge." I guess my diet falls somewhere between vinaigrette salad dressing and dressing an elk for the fire pit.

For anyone who's experienced fruitless days searching for a decent rental on Santa Fe/ Taos Craigslist, you may have noticed that your diet sometimes falls as a pre-requisite whim of the landlord. One rental requested a "humane eater." In laymen terms it means the landlord expects her tenant to lay off the bacon. Therefore the tenant would never use his own frying pan to serve up a beefy stuffed poblano pepper in the casita for which rent was paid. I'm pretty certain if you ask an attorney, (as Reddit often suggests) such a dietary request is unlawful tenant discrimination. Even the half bankrupt airlines make attempts to appease the gastro needs of all passengers. Go for the kosher meals when flying, they are the freshest, or at minimum order any special diet meal suitable for vegetarians or the Jain religion.

    I retorted to a poster who requested that potential tenants adhere to a specific diet. It was my American Civil Liberties Union moment. On Santa Fe Craigslist you're more likely to get a response talking about politics or diet rather than sharing a photo of your crotch.

    Aside from me lamenting that the landlord shouldn't rent out a property if they are requiring a tenant to abide by dietary customs, and asking that the tenant meditate regularly, I made an innocent comment about how eating locally sourced meat can be healthy. Angry comments awaited me within the hour. I was chewed out (pun intended) about how ignorant my locally and grass raised sourced meat eating claims were.

    Off-grid living can migrate toward the revived trend of homesteader lifestyles that include gutting, skinning and tanning one's livestock. Or it can take the path of a pure plant based diet, opting to live sans fridge while growing quinoa and kale. Even with these seemingly opposite perspectives, both are poised on a desire to tread lightly on the planet and achieve more self-reliance.

    In contemplating self-reliance and homegrown food, I'm interested in how many of us can actually live life without access to a grocery store and live one hundred percent "off the land." Because of our comfort level in the US, faced with a prolonged emergency, I imagine our civilized world will crumble quickly resulting in riots and a return to barbarianism when the food trucks fail to arrive. FEMA will not always be around the corner. Remember people can now get a multitude of fast food grub delivered to their homes and offices with the push of a button. Because there's significant demand for the service there are several companies who will deliver your mouth watering craving in a hot insulated bag. It is the complete opposite of tossing seeds in the ground and two months later hoping something tasty sprouts out of the soil.

Regardless of dietary preference, virtually anyone desirous of an off-grid lifestyle wants a vegetable garden and greenhouse. Some folks are born with a green thumb or hope that one day they can keep a plant alive. Foodie blogs boast photographs of their homegrown bounty featuring heirloom tomatoes. Rarely are photos of failed crops posted. It's such an earthy experience to pull a giant zucchini off the vine and make fritters or pasta sauce with your own harvested tomatoes. It's as primal an experience as sharing pictures of your newborn or puppy.

This past summer I experimented and grew a few beans and tomatoes. It wasn't enough for a pot of chili, nor a side dish. My tomatoes, even with mushroom compost, failed to reach epic proportions to run an Italian eatery. My beans grew into new beans, but it was a paltry quantity with nothing left for a long winter ahead. At the time of this writing, I am thankful that grocery stores still exist so I can buy supplemental tomatoes when things go wrong at home with my tomato plants.

Like building a house, gardens take a lot of planning and maintenance to scale up, which is another full time job when the goal is feeding yourself and possibly others. When everything goes right, you will have canned your bounty for winter consumption. Granted, doing this sort of work is so much more fulfilling than the majority of life draining day jobs.

There's a big difference between growing a few tomato plants and feeding your family exclusively for an extended time from your idyllic vegetable garden. If your aim is to be a year around forager, omitting all animal protein (even a fish), you'll still need a "state of the art" commercial sized greenhouse that can accommodate your veggie diet through the winter months, or perhaps it's possible to double your canning and jarring quota. Without a garden, if you're the nomadic sort who is an exclusive forager you will encounter what other survivalists attest: foraging is a seasonal endeavor.

A squirrel can pack her checks, hoarding her nut cash that nourishes her two-pound body through snowstorms. For a human to live on nut butter year around, well, that's a lot of nuts. I just don't think it's possible to live on a vegan diet and be self-reliant in the strictest since of the word. Vegetarianism is doable, but even then, there will be challenges growing grains beside a quaint cabin of northern latitude. As a full time farmer, you won't answer to a boss, but you will be at the mercy of the weather.

Eating off-grid suggests reducing your garbage output because that means another trip to the transfer station or burning trash on the homestead you call Ranchette Kumbaya. When you live off-grid, you probably won't have refuse service or you are the frugal individual who will haul your trash to the dump rather than paying for pick up service. You could bury your trash, but even that will take some time away from other off-grid chores and goals. Theoretically being a TEOTWAWKI (the end of the world as we know it) or SHTF (shit-hits-the-fan) planner, you won't rely on refuse service anyway because you seek self-sufficiency and anonymity.

Like camping and hiking in pristine areas, the leave no trace philosophy applies here. That means getting rid of all your own trash without help and without becoming a junkyard hoarder. You don't want to be that loner with the trash heap that lives down the road or the guy who periodically has a dark, noxious plume of smoke rising from his property.

Utilities Nearby

One way some people reduce their rubbish is to take the vow of living plastic free. It's an honorable endeavor coming full circle off packaged foods, impulse purchases and the sad swirling plastic garbage heap drifting across the Pacific Ocean. The plastic free concept goes well with the European trend for zero waste grocery stores. Giving up on buying boxes of plastic wrapped pizza bites must be an achievable goal. Those serious about reducing their garbage aren't hauling their yogurt cups to the recycle dumpsters. They either forgo yogurt all together, they buy locally made yogurt that comes in a glass container, or they make yogurt at home by raising their own livestock.

Self-sufficiency is often equated with storing a warehouse full of beans and rice. From this back stock of beans, will millions more be grown? Because when I emerge from my underground bunker, I won't be able to go shop for more beans. I'll have to hope for bartering with remaining survivors and I better have some mighty fine swag to trade, like a fully roasted turkey. At this point, I probably won't care about beans. More likely I'll make spears to intimidate and loot supplies from other hunter gathers.

Here in New Mexico, aside from maintaining a herd of cattle, one strategy to a sustainable protein source is to install a small pond in the home and stock it with fish. Move over backyard chickens! In the future perhaps micro-at-home fisheries will be more popular than micro-breweries. After all, drinking beer goes best with fatty appetizers like hot wings, breaded mozzarella sticks and other high calorie finger foods. The sort of foods I like to eat when I emerge from the woods after a strenuous hike.

In the blogosphere, an unnamed survivalist touted the carefree utopian vision of maintaining a stocked fish tank in the sunroom of her future Earthship. However, this idea was still hypothetical and her current city home was far from New Mexico. It all sounded plausible without pondering a lot of the practical details. It is similar to watching a

YouTube video of someone chopping wood and then actually going outside to chop wood. Quickly your office limp arms can't put out more energy and your heart is pounding. Recall that some people die of heart attacks shoveling snow. But fitness levels can always be improved upon and chopping wood is a matter of brute strength and efficient skill compared with the intricacies of fish farming.

There are a variety of fish that can potentially be raised in an indoor aquaculture environment and tilapia ranks as one of the best species to consider. The knowledge it takes to run a bountiful tilapia farm is quite extensive. How do you feed your fish in the apocalypse to keep them breeding fast enough to sustain your belly and your home fishery?

I started doing some figures based on several tilapia farming websites: Each one pound fish needs nearly four gallons of water to live a content life without feeling crowded, which would compromise their immune systems, well being and growth. I calculated that a 750 gallon tank measuring around 7' x 3' would hold about 150 happy swimming 1lb tilapia fish. I reduced the total by approximately 20% assuming a few fish would not make it to maturity. It takes about 265 days to grow a tilapia to one pound.

Next consider filtration and fresh water. Gray water systems are not an option because tilapia should only swim in potable water you yourself are willing to drink. I started wondering about water catchment systems and the allocation of water for tilapia farming verses another off-grid activity. If my theoretical property didn't have a live water source or a well, what percentage of my potable water would support the fish? In addition, I need to filter the water constantly and provide enough light using off the grid energy to maintain healthy fish.

Assuming my husband and I decided we would never entertain and we only ate a single 1 lb. fish each per day, we would run out of fish in a little over 2 months. Yet, it would take over 8 months to replenish our original 150 tilapia fish.

Utilities Nearby

If we share one fish per day, our supply would last about 5 months, still not enough to replace our original quantity. If we ate 3 fish per week, that would be 150 tilapia consumed over 11+ months thus allowing time to replenish our fish farm without depleting stock. Being mostly vegetarian while eating some fish could generate a fully independent food supply under this model. It can also be off set with stream fishing, other farming or eating other animals that could supplement our self-sufficient bliss. So perhaps, the theory of small-scale fish farming at home could work. The whole circle of life theory comes together after I skim the nutrient rich fish poop out of the stock tank and add it to the garden.

There's one last food and body product that must be discussed in relationship to the self-sustaining life and that is coconut oil. Geographically, living in the mountain desert on a remote New Mexico mesa, you must wean yourself off coconut oil right now. That means no more smearing it on your hair, eyebrows, strange skin aliments or eating it by the spoonful for a healthy sheen.

The climate zones of New Mexico simply do not make growing coconuts feasible. Many natural moisturizing products (including being a cheap skate who uses organic vegetable shortening) originate with plants from the tropics. Palm oil and shea butter grow in warm climates. Even if I could build a climate controlled green house and grow my own palm and shea trees, it will be years before I'll be able to harvest a coconut. Unless you are fine using petroleum products, this means that you're going to have to live without or moisturize with a locally available alternative, like sheep lanolin, olive oil, nut oils, bees' wax or used restaurant grease.

In the southern part of New Mexico, the hot deserts grow our famous green chiles along with pecans, pistachios, the ocotillo and even olives. North of Albuquerque, which is the line in the sand for virtually all plant life in the state, the aforementioned crops are not well adapted to the sunny, yet frigid winters. It's just too cold. Nuts and olive oil are two incredibly nourishing foods that also work well for homemade body products. They make great substitutes to coconut oil if your endeavor is being self-reliant and animal product free in an off-grid New Mexico life. To achieve this, you'll fair better in Las Cruces over the Santa Fe climate if your goal is to generate all of your own food and beauty products without keeping any animals.

As much as we love guacamole, it's just not possible to grow healthy avocados in New Mexico's arid climate. Forget about slathering on a homegrown avocado facemask when you reach the back forty. A word of advice from the purists, please do not add mayonnaise to your guacamole. The avocado is a true miracle food, successful even at making vegan chocolate mousse, you'll never know the difference. In your off-grid life however, unless you can green house it with humidity, the avocado will not be part of your self-reliant New Mexico lifestyle. To grow avocados you'll have to move to the more tropical zones of Mexico.

New Mexico encompasses the beauty of mountain desert paired with slivers of alpine forest. Choosing to live off-grid in the northern part of the state substantially shifts the kinds of crops you'll be able to grow on your own. There is still diversity in corns and other vegetables long cultivated by the first nations in the northern part of the state. People flourished for millennia perfectly fine, sans electricity and European influx. If you're willing to raise dairy goats or sheep, the ability to achieve a largely independent lifestyle in northern New Mexico is a real possibility. Goats tie into an incredibly diverse range of the world's cultures and climates from Asia, Africa to the Diné people. Goats are also better equipped to extract nutrients off desert shrubbery that cattle will not eat.

Having access to eggs is a massive nutritional source and a diversity of foods (i.e., breakfast burritos) are possible

UTILITIES NEARBY

with the humble egg. Raising backyard chickens has given many urban people the opportunity to experience farming. But again, a chicken doesn't magically out put eggs on demand and eventually she stops producing long before her natural life is over. This means you'll need more than a few chickens and you'll need a rotation of young chickens to compensate for your beloved retired hens. The stewards of backyard chickens are then faced with letting the hens live out their natural life as pets or applying the more gruesome life and death chores often dealt to the farm kids of history.

I recall someone once telling me that she did not eat anything that had a face. This contrasted with another woman I met this past year who as a homesteader, shared her experience of killing, plucking and preparing her own home raised chickens. For her it was a practical, spiritual and time consuming process. It was something I had a difficult time fathoming myself doing as I recalled hanging out with chickens, but not actually being responsible for their demise.

I had been a faux farmer, a pet sitter, carrying around a bantam hen with a name, inside my jacket while she clucked and ate out of my hand. I had photographed people's pets, sharing a carrot with a pot-bellied pig and thinking about how a pig's organs are so similar to our own. I'd had a pet guinea pig that lived eight healthy years before dying peacefully next to a yarrow plant in the yard, having eaten numerous red leaf lettuce bushels bigger than her own body. She never became the Peruvian cuye dish, she was my pet.

Anyone intrigued enough to plan for life and eating off-grid will abut these ideas and questions. Eventually, the great majority of dietary self-sufficiency rounds it's way back to bartering with our fellow humans. Which is why in the off-grid nation, New Mexico will have green chile to trade in exchange for coconut oil. One day after having spent years on a mesa eating home raised fish, chicken, eggs, veggies and goat's milk, someone will remember that there's a world out there with chocolate, coffee, cardamom, coconut pie, citrus fruits and tequila. No one technically needs any of these nutritional resources to survive, but we sure enjoy them.

The reality is that when it comes to self-reliance regarding what we eat, it's unlikely anyone can survive on a vegan lifestyle year around unless you reside in the tropics. That's why the people in Hawaii who don't eat Spam are wearing flip-flops year around, talking about mango smoothies and juicing. They aren't huddled under a blanket foraging like a grizzly bear for extra fat. This is particularly true when living through cold winters and you need to keep warm to stay alive. In this situation you might not be able to forgo a wool sweater or a hide to sleep on. At the same time, your physical lifestyle will require oodles of calories and that probably means consuming an animal product.

Still it would be difficult for me to hunt an animal or watch a fish gasping for breath or pluck my own dead chicken. It is sometimes said that if you can't stomach such events you should never eat meat. In the quest for life off the grid, how you plan to eat plays a significant factor in what self-sufficiency means to you. I don't fault people who are capable of being vegan for years at a time. I don't fault others for eating the occasional hamburger. Regardless of dietary choice, most of us see the need to step away from industrialized farming. That is something we all must do to ethically and sustainably survive together on this planet and it's something off-grid life offers.

Faced with growing all of your own food you might not have a day job anymore because there simply are not enough hours in the day to manage all of your own food production and do anything else. That is a radical decision and I admire people who possess the skills and drive necessary to commit to such a way of life. As an insurance policy on our own lives, it's good idea to have friends that can

Utilities Nearby

fish and perhaps even hunt when foraging is slim pickings or canning back stock is minimal. With the exception of remote tribal societies, very few modern people can produce all of their own food and the ones that are capable of doing so live a life that even digital nomads can't fathom. With the physical labor and time involved, one ends up relying on the mutual assistance of a few other people, even a loosely defined community.

If basing your diet off backcountry life is your calling, than read about Richard Proenneke. He was a true backcountry man living for several decades in Alaska, albeit still originating from the "lower 48." I'll always remember an ex-boyfriend from upstate New York that dreamed of raising bison out west and who introduced me to the 2004 documentary about Proenneke, *Alone in the Wilderness*.

There is a large proportion of the population who don't want to spend their day carving a spoon out of wood, but there are also plenty of people who believe they want to live the Proenneke dream too. That means forgetting about the pizza place down the road, unless you are actually on a wilderness T.V. show pretending to hack it off-grid. When filming ends, you can drive a mile on a paved road back to the pizza place.

THE LEW WALLACE CURSE OF NEW MEXICO

"All calculations based on our experiences elsewhere fail in New Mexico."
-Lew Wallace, Governor of New Mexico 1878 to 1881

"You could be renting in New York City."
- Ex-New Yorker

Diane, an ex-New Yorker just arrived in the Land of Enchantment and for the first time in her life she saw a western sunset. Years before that she had an incredible walk up apartment in New York City. It was one of the last rent-controlled apartments in Manhattan and she secured the lease back in the 1970's before I was born. Diane reminisces about the days of rent control in Manhattan when she found her first apartment. It was on Forty-something street between 6th and 7th avenue. She tells me the story again:

"It wasn't a great apartment, but it was clean and had wood floors. If you stretched your neck you could see the ball drop in Time Square…Wow! You remember the details," she says as I finish her sentence in this version of the story.

Utilities Nearby

Diane goes on, "At the time I was commuting from Long Island, I got up at 4:00 am to catch the early morning train. It was hell. While I looked for an apartment, I stayed at my friend's pad in Manhattan, which was a ghetto. It was full of cockroaches and perverts. You've got to remember that New York in the 1970's and 80's was a dirty, dangerous place."

I counter, "Yeah, I remember reading that Malcolm Gladwell book about crime in New York back then and how the city finally cracked down on slums and graffiti."

"Well" says Diane, "Every weekend I went down to get the first paper off the press and perused the apartments section. It was terrible because there was nothing in my price range and even if there was, I had to hurry because all the good apartments were rented by 10:00 that morning."

"The same thing happened when my cousin moved to New York after college," I say. "She lives in Hell's Kitchen. Her place is a hell hole, I don't even think it qualifies as an apartment. She found a room with a hot plate after getting a liberal arts degree from a small private college. She works near Union Square and lives on ninety-nine cent pizza."

Diane interjects while swirling her wine glass, "Back in my day Hell's Kitchen was a ghetto. Now it's up and coming." Diane pauses, "Well," she says, "You shouldn't live in New York. New York will hate you and grind you into little pieces. You should move to San Francisco, or Athens, Georgia. REM is from Athens, Georgia. It's a college town. You're still young, you'd like it."

I dismiss Diane's advice, "I'm not really sure where we will move, but it will be near a hub airport and on the grid."

In that moment I'm imagining the perfect corporate job some place beyond New Mexico, where I'll forget about my entrepreneurial goals, green chile and sunsets while shoehorning myself into a crummy condo in a city that has big companies and staffing agencies. Being practical means I really should leave this State, everyone else with a college degree is leaving in droves, why should I stay here?

I look across the table at Diane. Smooth jazz radio plays in the background and one of her cats is rubbing against my feet. Although Diane only recently moved to Santa Fe, she espoused expertise about finding an adobe rental. It was difficult for her to relate to my personal plight because she was retired and lived on the grid with her cats in a semi-detached stucco bungalow that was paid for in full.

It's still worth mentioning that Diane currently illegally sublets her perfect New York apartment and can't quite let go of the lease. In the end, Diane had no recommendations of affordable places for my generation that grew up around Santa Fe and wanted to stay. Instead she regaled me with advice that only worked in New York.

"In New York, disgruntled renters turn up the heat prior to moving out of their apartment; put the radiator on full blast when you vacate your place—that will teach the landlord a lesson," says Diane.

If I had an oil radiator heater I would have. Getting advice from an ex-New Yorker in Santa Fe is like gritting your teeth and drinking ten cups of coffee to power through it. You want the opportunity and promotion. Since you live on a mesa in New Mexico you never get to network with the well-connected east coast agencies and businesses. Meeting a recent New York transplant that just arrived in Santa Fe, who might know "someone" could be worth your while. It means you could have the best of both worlds—living in beautiful New Mexico and still being a player in the game of life.

I apologize for stereotyping New Yorkers here. It's no different than making the sweeping claim that everyone in Orange County, California votes republican. There are some great New Yorkers I just don't keep in touch with them anymore, although my husband used to work with quite a few in the art sector. They used to ask why my husband didn't move to New York City until they visited Santa Fe. "Oh," they would say, "I can see why you stay in New Mexico."

Several years ago, on a miserable trip to New York City in which I embarked on a miserable trade show at Javits Convention Center, my husband and I spent one free day wandering around The Metropolitan Museum of Art and a few galleries owned by people who once knew him. Up the elevator of what appeared to be a gold gilded building, small talk ensued at a gallery that was far from memorable. The topic of rent for galleries popped up and the answer for this space was, "Thirty." We hardly had to ponder if $3000 was implied because it was most likely $30,000 a month just to hang a little bit of art on the wall.

After that trip I swore that I would unequivocally never visit New York City ever again. My husband doesn't speak in such severe absolutes as I, so I mashed in the depth of my feelings. Even if I made the *New York Times Best Seller* list and was *Sex in the City* successful, I will never again visit New York City. It was the most miserable time of my life next to the professionally unfulfilling years of my life living in New Mexico. So most likely, since the rest of my life will be unequivocally unsuccessful, I will remain unfulfilled right here. At least in New Mexico, I'll have a modicum of comfort in fresh air, sunsets and eating. Be sure to consider me as an inspiring speaker for the next graduating class commencement speech.

Around the time of my fated New York City trip, Diane decided she wanted to date again, but she didn't want to date another ex-New Yorker. We talked about her dating options over her bastardized homemade frito pie in which she pulverized the beans and Frito chips in a blender. It was time to get online and take a few test date spins. More First Fridays ensued, only these were Santa Fe First Fridays with few studs and one ex-convict. Diane couldn't help noticing that the restaurants around here closed earlier than in New

York. I gave Diane a few pointers on planning her Christmas cocktail party, like the fact that although people are willing to stand in New York, people in Santa Fe like to sit down. By the time Diane's Christmas cocktail party rolled around, it seemed she had had enough of Santa Fe mañana.

My friendship with Diane, the transplanted New Yorker ended because of an incessant conversation about Tesla. Over the holidays Diane had visited her relative who picked her up at LAX in a Tesla.

Tesla was the most L.A. thing since veganism and Diane couldn't get enough. "They have these power up stations across the country" she told me over a cup of tea. "You must go test drive a Tesla, it will change your life." A few days later Diane emailed me multiple times about the merits of Tesla, even contacting her relative to c.c. me on an email with a testimonial about how much his life had improved since buying a Tesla. Tesla had become Diane's personal savior and like that friend that suddenly goes evangelical, it was becoming too much.

Diane had never owned a car until just this past year when she relocated from New York City to New Mexico. She couldn't understand how many hours it took to drive across Texas. I agreed that like solar panels, Tesla technology would improve, eventually replacing the horse and buggy still popular in New Mexico. But by then the friendship was over and it was all because I wouldn't go test drive a Tesla. Actually, it was because I didn't want to see a certain Academy Award winning film, but that's the thing about transplants in Santa Fe. They want to force you into liking something that never mattered to you and they just got here from a crowded, polluted yet stylish city that smells of urine.

New Mexico may have lost the new Tesla Gigafactory to Nevada, but that doesn't stop our State from fruitlessly attempting to bring something to New Mexico—besides importing Californians to work in the film industry for tax write offs while hiring three New Mexicans as Production Assistants. Now humble Los Lunas is slated to be New Mexico's developing Silicon Valley all because Facebook moved in. Since the announcement, rental properties are already appearing that cost a few hundred more since last year and that tout being "near Facebook." I guess artist Judy Chicago's move to Belen years ago will finally pay off between Facebook and the sparse schedules of the Rail Runner train. Let's not get started on Albuquerque's Rapid Transit project on historic Route 66.

Don't move to New Mexico because it will make you cool or because you are lost. This state doesn't have an interest in what's going on elsewhere or what's in vogue and that's fine. I'm sure the Tesla works great for those driving around California or Connecticut but this is New Mexico. It reminded me of the time I visited Hacienda de los Martinez, now a beautiful living museum in Taos. There on a placard read: Train at Servilleta: Throughout Don Serverino Martinez's life there was little hard cash to be found in New Mexico. This was at the turn of the 19th century and I felt the same as Don Serverino Martinez had experienced two centuries prior.

In the end Martinez did achieve success in farming and trade at the northern terminus of the Camino Real, all while raising six children and before the first solar panels were invented. It makes me reconsider my aforementioned whining on electric kettles. By all means, I recommend taking the time to explore New Mexico's museums. Places such as Hacienda de los Martinez and El Rancho de las Golondrinas will give visitors the embodied experience of authentic adobe architecture compared to modern equivalents. These are homes built and lived in long before the availability of modern electricity.

Contrary to what a few readers might think about me, I don't work for an oil company. I'm not a transplant from a big city and I've never lived in a penthouse. The rest of you either embrace my unsolicited perspectives or call me a sustainable party-pooper. Some could even call me anti-propane. Garden pitchforks are pointed at me on both sides: the sun loving people vs. hail fossil fuels people. I'm somewhere in the middle. In fact back in my 20's when I dreamed of going off-grid I tried my hand at buying a minuscule amount of stock in a solar company. So far that stock hasn't paid off and it's probably because of my Craigslist post lamenting about a solar power rental property.

Like Fox News, this book aims to be fair and balanced, so I'll make a positive plug for the solar companies: Here in New Mexico solar power does work and it works better here than just about any other place in the US. Keep in mind solar power technology is always improving. Solar is renewable. It doesn't require obliterating Alaskan wildlife to drill out the last vestiges of fossil fuel. As one Craigslist letter reminded me, there are wonderful experiences to be had living close to nature. Being aware of your energy usage is beneficial to the planet. These are things to consider. Cutting back on electricity use is possible, particularly if you are simply living off-grid, rather than working and living off-grid.

I'm not here to slam self-professed hippies either. Carol, my Peace Corp friend of the 1960's says, "Give me a blanket and a backpack and I'm good to go." A true vagabond still on the go, this is her definition of home needs. Her dog's passport is enviable. Carol only regrets not buying a casita in San Miguel de Allende before the gringos thought the quaint Mexican town made a glorious expat community. There Carol rents a small place and hangs out with a resident Chihuahua. She's not responsible for the upkeep or taxes on the property and can keep exploring the world.

Allow let me to plug real estate brokers so when I make an appearance at Tune Up Café and run into my real estate friend, she can still like my book. There could be real estate agents miffed by my take on Santa Fe real estate, but I'm

Utilities Nearby

certain I've lived in more Santa Fe homes including those off-grid than the average real estate broker. It's not the real estate agent's fault that a home is in a prime location and needs updating. Like any salesperson, a real estate agent describes whatever property they are selling in the most desirable terms. Sometimes it means focusing on the theoretical possibilities of a property.

Writing a property description means tugging at the heartstrings of buyers, glossing over perceived problems and being a glass is half-full kind of person. It's far easier to talk about starry skies and Rancho dreams than to acknowledge the fact that raw land is exactly that. Saying a property exists under the guise of "sensible covenants" is a tidy way of saying it's what any normal person would choose, even you.

A few people have told me I should go into real estate or wondered if I already had. Thank you. This book is my version of "going into real estate" without paying for a real estate license or having a down payment. It is dipping my toe in the proverbial desert waters of property management, home buying and building. I love real estate in all its forms from zoning to HGTV.

I can even navigate the grit about resolving landlord/tenant disputes. It could be something basic like a broken appliance or as death defying as a neighbor's bullet lodged in a shared apartment wall. The latter is not theatrics, but a true story. The first step for justice seeking individuals is to document the wrongs done unto them in an effort to compile a legal case. Small claims court is the American way. Again you write a notarized letter to your landlord:

> *It has come to my attention that the dryer in Unit 4B no longer retains the ability to dry clothing. Will you please send a maintenance person?*

- Your Reliable Tenant

The reply from the landlord is hopeless:

Dear Unit 4B,

Hang up a line because the dryer was not part of the lease. Consider it more of an unnecessary amenity. Take it over to the laundromat that requires forty quarters a load. P.S. That dryer worked perfectly fine for over a decade until you moved in, so kiss your deposit goodbye.

Sincerely,

The Landlord

    In the end it will all work out. While doing laundry in town you might meet an intellectual, cultured partner and fall madly in love. Just think about how it will be a broken dryer and your landlord's sluggish indifference that ultimately made your life meaningful.
    Going to small claims court is like saying you can still renew your post office box at the old rate even though the post office arbitrarily adjusted the annual rate mid month and your box wasn't up for renewal until the following month. Had your payment been received just a couple days earlier you would have saved ten dollars. Simple tasks that seem straight forward can sometimes take hours. As other disgruntled tenants point out, the Landlord Hot Line service is no longer free due to budget cuts and most likely, you'll be told to hire an attorney.
    Just because you win a small claims judgment doesn't mean the landlord will shell out the cash you deserve. Those without a conscience (and this applies not only to landlords) will feign hardship, sick relatives, and other pressing matters in an effective attempt to delay a payout to a tenant. It won't be free for the tenant to exercise this injustice either and the outcome will typically be a few hundred dollars,

maybe a grand or two. Bleeding out on righteousness may or may not be worth the energy. Some say the same thing about writing a book.

Although much of this book is about dooms day and my persistent agitated depression, I am a fan of positive language framing in the genre of the linguist George Lakoff. When I go to the store and buy a giant plastic storage bin, I notice how the sign reads, "Don't forget the lid" instead of the positive "Remember the lid." Please excuse the swath of "don'ts" that follow. I promise to look on the bright side in the next paragraph.

My first off-grid sojourn was a mistake and after enough emotional freedom tapping, it's a mistake I've learned to accept. Learn your lesson not to rent from Stephen King's Annie Wilkes. But first don't get a liberal arts degree. Don't assume you will breeze through writing your novel in off-grid serenity rather than inside a micro-apartment in New York City. Become an artist and live that way for at least a decade before you move to an "art town." People come out west all the time to pursue a new career in art.

Never assume that magnificent vistas will inspire you to be more of a go-getter. Don't stumble upon people who don't want to be found or expect that you will find yourself. Don't trash hippies. Don't join groups because you are lonely and want to meet people in a new town. In a small town, you'll meet people soon enough and it's hard grocery shopping where you run into people you've already met. Don't move to New Mexico and make negative remarks about Mexicans and illegals or how you want a border wall. Don't be the "whiney guera" like me. Don't dampen the dreams of others, it might be all they have left. Most definitely don't tell people living off the grid in New Mexico is a terrible idea. After all, I have a certified New Mexico True company and the tourism department needs my support. So please come enjoy a margarita with me.

Do come visit New Mexico, maybe even move here. Look beyond Santa Fe too. Do consider life off the grid, just bring a can-do attitude and research what it really takes to be comfortable. Do be open to all the cultures that make up New Mexico. Do support the local restaurants and independent businesses. Do donate to the diverse non-profits of New Mexico and volunteer your time. Do come to The Horse Shelter's annual spring fundraiser. Do go camping and hiking around the state. Do adopt a dog or cat here, we have a lot of homeless pets. Do support education for New Mexico's kids. Do teach a class. Do learn about the history of New Mexico. Do come here and make something beautiful. Do occasionally engage with your community even if you really love solitude most of the time. Do eat an authentic frito pie. Oh, and do continue writing letters to the editor.

I didn't find John Muir or write the great American novel on a mesa. I was too cold. It's a terrible excuse, I know. Today, I finally finish writing this book and the view out my window isn't of Santa Fe, it's a chain link fence, a ream of barbed wire and a guy's reclaimed curb alert armchair parked in an alley, but I'm still here. There's a mangled plastic bag caught on the barbed wire and a towering electric pole, but the great things about this state are right beyond this view.

When I worked in downtown Santa Fe, tourists to New Mexico would tell me how lucky I was to live here, how much they had enjoyed their visit to Santa Fe and staying in the hotels I couldn't afford. Then we would talk about green chile and sunsets and adobe while eating California salad.

In the end, I have stayed in New Mexico, flitting out several times into the rest of the world. Knowing that things like phone service and public transport actually work in those other places, but even the curse of Lew Wallace wouldn't make me leave New Mexico. I plan to spend the

Utilities Nearby

rest of my life here and to improve my outlook after a couple of incredibly challenging years. Always I remember hiking at sunset with the great dogs of my life and the new ones too in spectacular quiet places where I only hear the ravens and the occasional coyote.

Home. It's a personal hide away where your belongings reflect you. It's a place out of town to have a bunch of dogs. It's simultaneously a place to entertain and a sanctuary to rejuvenate away from the world. It's my unsolicited opinion to those of you lurking on an enchanted mesa in New Mexico (or who dream of doing so), that thermostats are personal preference. As the dust billows behind your car on a washboard New Mexico road, each of you, and only you will know whether you're getting the hell out or you're just on your way home.

GLOSSARY OF SANTA FE REAL ESTATE TERMS

ACEQUIA
Mentioned in real estate listings that appear on the east side of Santa Fe and Canyon Road.

ARROYO
Mentioned in real estate listings that appear where mobile homes and campers are allowed.

ADOBE
Clay mud mixed with a small amount of straw. Not to be confused with "strawbale." These sun-baked bricks are the essence of every true casita and hacienda.

BANCO
A built in bench made of stucco. In most houses the banco is typically decorative, narrow and not lounge worthy for sitting. However, the traditional "shepherd's bed" is a wide banco similar to an XL twin at a college dorm, only more tranquil.

CANALE
Use this to channel rainwater off your flat roof into a rain barrel.

COYOTE FENCE
A vertical stick fence authentic to New Mexico. True coyote fence will be of uneven heights. HOA compliant coyote fence will be trimmed on top to appear uniform.

HACIENDA
Any stucco building that is not an efficiency casita apartment. Sometimes referred to as a family or artist compound.

UTILITIES NEARBY

HOA
People who meddle in the affairs of others and don't understand authentic New Mexico.

HORNO
An outdoor oven made from adobe.

KIVA
A stucco fireplace outside or inside, typically located in the corner of a room with or without a banco.

STRAWBALE
Remedial knowledge of stacking strawbales. Similar to playing Lincoln Logs when you were a kid except there are no pre-cut notches. This requires reams of chicken wire.

PASSIVE SOLAR
An authentic New Mexico home built before HOA's were invented. It has southern exposure, big windows and most likely electricity with baseboard heaters for those days that are cloudy unless it's off grid.

NICHO
A small triangular recessed shelf built into a plastered wall suitable for showcasing a Buddha statue, an urn, or a Retablo from Spanish Market.

SATILLO TILE
Any red-orange tile that looks like the real thing from Mexico only it's ceramic (not terra cotta) and it was made in China, but people love the up sell. Tourists innocently call it "Terra Cotta."

LATILLAS
Small wooden sticks that go across the ceiling.

TONGUE & GROOVE (T&G) CEILINGS
Square wooden beams that go across the ceiling.

VIGAS
Logs that go across the ceiling.

OFF-GRID LOT
There is no electricity and probably won't be any for another century. Good chance there's no water or septic either. Euphemistically referred to as "raw land."

NEIGHBORHOODS OF SANTA FE, NEW MEXICO

ARTIST ROAD
You could call it a "condo" maybe with a stacked washer-dryer. It's practically 10,000 Waves Spa but with less parking and no hot tub. Still, it's close to skiing and the plaza.

SANTA FE/DOWNTOWN
Your "pied-a-terre" in adobe. (Note: It is very difficult for me to use "pied-a-terre" when describing Santa Fe real estate). Possibly your dream VRBO, Air B&B, Short Term Cash Cow, but remember the Historic District will want to tell you who you can and cannot date.

SANTA FE EAST SIDE
You just moved here from out of state or your family arrived centuries ago with the Conquistadors. Surprisingly, famed Canyon Road can look like a ghost town at certain times of the year making you wonder why you bought an art gallery. Those of you who are new to town and/or spiritual/vegetarian will enjoy the Upaya Zen Center on Cerro Gordo. The rest of us want to go back in time to when there were more goats and less Buddhists.

SANTA FE NORTH SIDE
The best dog park in the whole world is here. It's the only dog park that actually works since it's a vast area of trails and a football field of weeds that used to be the city dump. You can live in Casa Solana in an old outdated (or updated) overpriced single car, single bath adobe home. But it's walking distance to La Montanita Co-op, which you love because you value shopping locally and your dog loves the dog park. If you want to keep heading north you can find a

"compound" off Tano Road and from there you can practically watch the Santa Fe Opera without leaving home.

SANTA FE RAILYARD

Infatuation of Seattle meets NYC meets Micro Brewery. What happened to free parking? OMG the REI store is brick! What happened to Sangre de Cristo Mountain Sports? At least The Ark Bookstore is still here. What is this place? I loathe conceptual art! Look! There's a farmers market so it's okay. It's a great place to raise kids. OMG we're in the minority raising kids in a retirement town. The ghosts of Sanbusco Center live because not everyone could move to the De Vargas Center. Around the corner someone once broke into my street parked car and stole my moderately priced REI Siesta sleeping bag, but I bought it in ABQ because I didn't believe an REI should ever be in Santa Fe.

SANTA FE SOUTH EAST

Saint John's College outlived College of Santa Fe because more of us should study the classics before moving into our dream adobe in the foothills. For everyone else there's Atalaya Trail and lots of dogs. Which makes tolerating a run in with a "Johnny" tolerable. It's still better than running into tourists from Wisconsin who ask for navigation advice while professing their dislike of dogs. Now you will tell Wisconsin just how weird and screwed up your hometown of Santa Fe is hoping they will never relocate. Other times your humanness will show through and you'll have a lovely brief conversation with a fellow hiker. You'll remember you still like people. Here you can actually watch a stunning sunset instead of looking at #sunsetsoftheworld. You'll remember why you gutted out your 20's in a retirement town and never left for a normal place.

SANTA FE SOUTH CAPITAL

It's like Midtown Manhattan with a triplex instead of high rises. You must like one bedrooms and sometimes even street parking. But it's so close to Wholefoods, Trader Joes and yoga class, who really cares if it's overpriced? You're happy to work three part-time service industry jobs to make it work.

SANTA FE/ AGUA FRIA

It's where Dave's Not Here cafe used to be and where once in a while there used to be a few shootings. Now it's Tune Up Café, which has excellent huevos rancheros. It's where hipster abuts chain link fences and project cars still make good landscaping. Your adobe may be a fixer upper but you will pay market value because the property "has good bones." It's practically the gentrified "Baca Street District."

SANTA FE/ BACA STREET

It all started with the café, Counter Culture. A great place to eat, but hindering progress puts me in the minority. Your adobe will be small and parking will be tight. Although you could end up in a more hip cargo container Live/Work environment but it will cost you… and then the HOA will kick you in the butt in the name of "Grounds maintenance" and they might not even like your dog. Could you really hang out with people like that? I was never a Baca Street girl even when I used to sit on my laptop there and use the free WiFi.

SANTA FE/SILER ROAD "ARTS DISTRICT

Trend Magazine named once ghetto industrial Siler road an "Arts District." This is where the starving artists who couldn't afford to live by the plaza made their wares. No one got a warehouse off Siler to be seen eating brunch. They went there to make stuff with machines and blowtorches. They went there because it was cheap. I should mention that it's still cheaper than TriBeCa and if you have a plumbing problem there's still space to park a Septic truck. (Yes, you'll be on city water, not a septic, but for illustrative purposes most residents of Santa Fe County know what a Septic truck looks like). Oh, and Meow. Wolf. Whatever…I will save my review for my Who-Cares-What-You-Have-To-Say-Art-Critic-Certificate.

SANTA FE/SECOND STREET
It's all about hip Live/Work spaces and crapped out adobes. This is a central location where you can be yourself and make pizza or run a yoga studio while you live in the efficiency upstairs. I used to eat late lunch at Chocolate Maven in the winter while waiting for the croissants to go half price at 3pm. It's close to the car rental place for a quick get-away in case you traded your car in for a scooter. There's also the place that used to allow dogs on the patio but no longer does.

SANTA FE/SIRINGO/RODEO ROAD
It's behind where Baillos used to be which is now Savers thrift store and behind Natural Grocers (which has since moved). It's also behind the times so it's more affordable and truly local. There's Java Joes and Joe's Diner. Your home will likely need updating and you'll wonder if it's really worth living in Santa Fe over a cheaper tract house in Rio Rancho.

SANTA FE/COMMUNITY COLLEGE AREA
These new Southwestern overpriced patio homes are a relief after spending all that time living in a fixer upper. It looks inviting but there's a good chance your dishwasher will break after one year and at least one toilet will also need pre-mature replacing. It will happen when you have guests visiting. You'll have a Xeriscaped patio. It's pleasant

Utilities Nearby

except when the lady next door smokes cigarettes and talks incessantly on her phone. When you park in the cul-de-sac along the sloping curb an angry "anonymous'" neighbor will leave a note on your windshield telling you that it's illegal to park there. You will have neighbors that are content eating at chain restaurants even though in Santa Fe there is absolutely no excuse to not eat at local restuaunts. And if you even think for moment that you can't afford Santa Fe's restaurants because you are paying for an overpriced inferior built Southwestern patio home, get over to Allsups Gas Station and grab a Chimichanga. Remember the taco sauce.

SANTA FE SOUTH SIDE/AIRPORT ROAD

Tribes Coffee House is now here (instead of downtown), which makes the south side doable. Plus your neighbor is green chile at Horseman's Haven and if you can't be bothered to cook, access to chile is more important than living in a good school district. The beige stucco strip malls are a turn off unless you're the type that enjoys wandering the aisles of Target instead of writing your novel. If you're a studio loving person you can live in the warehouses off Airport road and it's still cheaper than California. Cool people still live here and it's not yet referred to as an "Arts District." Even legends of the *Santa Fe Reporter* once had a futon in these parts.

SANTA FE/OSUNA ROAD

It's a small adobe "bungalow" with a tiny bathroom. It reminds you of California because the house isn't really worth the asking price, but it's centrally located. The roof was just replaced fifteen years ago, which in New Mexico time is practically yesterday. There's even a shed in the backyard to store your extra crap because the one car garage was converted into a studio/bedroom/Air B&B. The greatest thing about this area is the park and dining at Red Enchilada, Baja Tacos and El Parasol.

SANTA FE WEST SIDE

Golf in Las Companas! You're a gated community kind of person and nature is a putting green. For most Santa Feans it's a Bermuda Triangle with nice houses and great views on the way to the Diablo Canyon trail head. But on the other side of HWY 599 you can still find some dirt road hideaways where no one will bother you too much. People outside the HOA zone will agree with you that golf courses are an environmentally unconscionable waste of water in the desert because this isn't Arizona.

TESUQUE

The real estate agents call it a "Pastoral Village in the foothills of the Sangre de Cristo Mountains ten minutes to the Plaza." It's beautiful and Four Seasons Resort is here. In short, there are plenty of "bring your imagination" properties and reclusive upscale hideaways for the misanthropic. There's Tesuque Market and you'll wish you were arriving on horseback instead of your new Subaru. (I swear this is my last joke about Subarus).

TURQUOISE TRAIL

This is where off the grid will make or break you. Half way through a property listing, like a tiny little bleep between "starry skies" and "horseback riding" will be two little words "off-grid." Will you do it? The realtors will tell you about all the western motorcycle movies made out here, true Tamalewood. I love Highway 14 and it was my teenage years fantasy while others dreamed of the prom. I still love Highway 14. Except Madrid... well, it's like trying to put a sweater on a feral cat. Real estate agents call it, "A quaint mining town turned artist haven." There's nothing really "quaint" about New Mexico. That would be Vermont. Madrid is really just a less expensive place to live where you may or may not be able to drink the water. In my opinion, I never said you couldn't drink the water, I said you might not *want* to). But Madrid is also like being Ted Danson in Cheers. "Sometimes you want to go where everybody knows your name." I probably won't want to go there after the "Madroids" read this. But Madroids, I definitely prefer you to Eldorado, doesn't everyone?

LAMY

Just don't. Hey there's Amtrak! Where's that Saloon? Is it open? Is it ever open? Is this place cursed? Is there a soda machine? Wasn't there a western wear photo shoot here once? Why is it so freaky? It's so seductively beautiful. My cell phone signal seems to have dropped. But wait, those people in the giant houses on the mesa top, the one's with electricity, they also have a Lamy address.

ELDORADO/OLD HOUSE

You used to shop at Wild Oats and drink reverse osmosis water. You still love Birkenstocks and astrology. You are especially fond of chickens. You never knew there was an HOA. At least two nice people live here, but not voluntarily. They are considering going off-grid to get away from the influx of new neighbors.

ELDORADO/NEW HOUSE

You just moved here from out of state and discover the open spaces make you uncomfortable. You enjoy the neighborhood newsletter Eldorado *Vistas*, especially the part about reporting neighbors who are violating the militant HOA.

TAOS

Your authentic adobe is a little cheaper than Santa Fe. There's the Taos hum. Your off-grid Eathship may or may not hum. So try an adobe with electricity nestled in the sagebrush. The pool in Taos is an oasis compared to the ghetto pools of Albuquerque. If you like to swim laps you can have your own lane without sharing it with a skinny hairy man in a Speedo. Hide out in the mountains of Taos Canyon. "Dude, where's your snow board? We're from back east." It's Boulder, Colorado minus the economy and spandex. Everything around here goes with Chaco Sandals and Patchouli (by the way, I still wear old Chaco Sandals. I also loved patchouli until my husband told me it was the smell of a hippie. I am a hypocrite). I love Taos because it's too far away from everything to be the epicenter of anything. Cid's grocery store and the Farmers' Market makes settling into Taos a real possibility. I have nothing against smoothies and or doing "soul work." Taos is whatever floats your high desert boat, like that Sam Elliott movie.

OTHER OUTLYING AREAS OF NORTHERN NEW MEXICO

Bring your yurt, camper, tiny house or log cabin kit. There may or may not be water. There may or may not be electricity. There may or may not be cell phone service or internet. The dirt road may or may not be maintained, but the vistas are stunning, the night skies are spectacular, the sagebrush is forever, the mountains are captivating, the junipers provide privacy, and you're still within range of green chile. In fact, in real estate terms you're just "minutes from area attractions." Like that grocery store you loathe shopping at because you always run into someone (especially the one time you're wearing your house clothes). There's a gas station around here with a great burrito. Out here it's like Santa Fe only a little cheaper and weirder. It's an hour or more to the Santa Fe plaza. Did you ever go there anyway? If you don't like it, California, Oregon, Texas and New York await your return. If you're staying, buy yourself a fleece vest that will be perpetually covered in dog hair.

ORIGINAL CRAIGSLIST POST

CAUTION OFF GRID SOLAR POWER RENTERS returns with that quirky inside Santa Fe Real Estate Edition: NEW TO SANTA FE? Must read! Remember readers this is about $ Value in Santa Fe/Taos Rentals (Not how to dehydrate food or push your fridge outside in the winter). Know before you RENT.

Somehow KWH are never mentioned, just low "Low Carbon Footprint." "Moderate Energy needs."

Love composting your own waste and running out of power? Spending hundreds on propane? All for $700-$1200+ a month! Hold on Serenity Seekers: Ask these questions BEFORE RENTING OFF GRID IN NM:

This post is about perceived value when a landlord offers an off grid property without informing newbies to NM (or newbies to off grid living) what it entails. Cost wise as a renter, you are not saving money. (Read: propane). Technically you are renting a property with 'implied habitability' but not really since off grid homes in Northern NM are frequently built with VERY limited 'solar/battery power', nor are they complete in their construction, nor are they comfortable places to inhabit in the winter.

Please learn from our experiences in renting off the grid! As you peruse Santa Fe/Taos rentals you'll notice many landlords are eager to rent their off the grid hovels in spring/summer. Picture the opening of Game of Thrones. It snows in Northern NM. This isn't LA and or Arizona.

Some of you folks from New Jersey or California suburban hell may be tempted by a beautiful off the grid property in NM. Off the grid homes look their best in moderate seasons- NOT WINTER. (Spare me "I sponge bathed all winter in a yurt and had the time of my life"). This is about $$. Except for those hippies who love over priced crappy Santa Fe rentals.

This post is about good questions you need to ask when renting off the grid. It's not an existential discussion about whether someone can lead a full life with or without a cappuccino machine or massage chair.

Don't be fooled by Adobe NM charm off the grid quiet just because it's SUNNY! Learn more about what to look for when renting OFF the Grid.

BONUS INFO: If a property says "Only utility renter pays is propane," this is a euphemism for "My house is freezing after October and it costs a butt load to keep warm".

NEW: Beware 'New Mexico Gray' exterior off grid / solar powered homes. This means they did it on the cheap and couldn't be bothered to put a top coat of stucco on the house. I have yet to see a more than a 75% done off grid home. It they didn't finish the outside, imagine what shortcomings you will discover upon move in.

NEW TO NEW MEXICO? Passive solar ON GRID home is NOT the same as OFF Grid "Solar Powered Country Home"

Cistern? A gallon of water weighs 8 lbs.

Forget about getting back your deposit or unused propane. Work in essential oils or Law of Attraction? Big red flag renters!

Utilities Nearby

Considering moving to Santa Fe or Taos? Ask the following questions before renting:

ASK: Can the off the grid home store 3-5 days of energy to get through cloudy days? This is standard for any habitable off grid home! Winter days means shorter hours of sunlight. Is the house oriented to the sun or is it positioned for 'views of expansive vistas'?

"SMALL Fridge" means underpowered--Especially in winter! Is the fridge propane or electric? This will make a big difference in your available electricity. Propane fridges cost more upfront, but it's the only time propane should be a part of your vocabulary when renting off the grid. It should NEVER be a heat source!

You need a minimum of 12 batteries MINIMUM. (NOT old ones!) Altitude also affects battery life AND solar panels wear out in the blazing mountain sun. This kind of system requires upkeep and cash to maintain. It's NOT a RonCo Cooker, "Just set it and forget it". Testing ratings for all solar panels and batteries are for sea level. NOT 7000' high altitude.

Propane Grid is NOT 'Off the Grid'. Make sure the house is actually PASSIVE SOLAR. Propane heat is a rip off! New Mexico is freezing in winter! Remember this! Propane man said the vented heaters get $.50 of heat for every $1 you pay. Propane heat smells. The un-vented ghetto wall heaters also have instructions saying to "Open the window an inch". This is counter-intuitive when it's 9 degrees outside. Yes, NM gets COLD in winter!

Do NOT do STRAWBALE. They have NO THERMAL MASS (like adobe or pumice) and are FREEZING IN WINTER! STRAWBALE also creates moldy, scratchy air.

Thick walls do NOT equal thermal mass (like Adobe or Pumice).

Avoid Earthships! The tires gas out as they decompose into the walls of the house. Sure it sounds great to be a 1970 hippie who built a mosaic wall of beer bottles, but patchouli oil doesn't keep the lights on.

Do NOT rent an off the grid home WITHOUT a WOODSTOVE! Remember this is STILL an 'interactive heat source', AKA "Rustic Charm". It's not like wearing a silk smokers robe and hitting a remote control to power up your fireplace in the living room while holding a cigar. (Why don't the hippies laugh at this part and take me so seriously?). It's true. Wood Stoves are great, but if it's your only heat source well, those are going to be some cold ass mornings--how much $$ are you paying? With a true passive solar home, most days you CAN be relatively comfortable.

SNOWING? If you are at work, your solar panels won't work covered in snow! ("bujj" sound of no power). Sweep those old solar panels with your snow broom while paying high rent for the 'nature experience'. If it's snowing all day, you'll have to get out there multiple times with your snow broom. It's like paying to be a caretaker of a property.

If you want internet and it goes out DO NOT EXPECT to get it fixed promptly because your internet will be through a Co-op of volunteers and NO ONE will come fix it in a timely manner. Or the whole system is old and out of date! If the house is already underpowered even worse. If you work from home like half of Northern NM this is an issue. And if you're a hippie preaching about "free internet at the library", that's a long way to town. No cell service? Yeah, you COULD get by.

Utilities Nearby

Sufficient electricity is required in any tenant agreement. If the home is NOT equipped with 'STATE OF THE ART SOLAR SYSTEM' (that means not installed by on the cheap hippies) and at least 12 batteries, forget it. How OLD is the system? The inverter. When was it last updated? You have to update this stuff every couple years and if you're not the owner, good luck with that!

When it's cold you can NOT plug in a wall heater! Forget it! It's a heat source appliance. Forget even looking at that HEAT DISH at the Hardware store.

HOW OLD ARE THE BATTERIES? Are they on the north (freezing) side of the house? BAD NEWS! You will lose a significant percentage of your short winter days charging because your batteries are freezing. Do they need to be watered? (Another task while you pay high rent).

Were the PVC water pipes (sticking out of the ground) dug deep enough so they don't freeze? Probably not by half the self-build hippies around here! We sure loved the frozen cast iron bathtub while sick with the flu and a landlord that opted to send an unlicensed plumber to the house.

DOES THE HOUSE HAVE A GENERATOR? Get ready for a loud noisy back up using fossil fuel self-sufficient queen! Or get ready to just run out of power, especially in the winter because you rented a house from someone that does not update their 'special system home' and does NOT have a generator with the house. Buy more candles; you WILL need them! Even on cloudy monsoon summer days!

A friend who does do ALL off the grid in a knowledgeable way with 15 batteries and huge solar array STILL does his laundry in town. Still does much of computer work in town.

LOOK at ALL items that plug in before you even think of off the grid self-sustainable living. You will be surprised! No toaster, no coffee pots no cappuccino, no hair dryers, no plug-in foot massage, no 'heat based' elements, no dishwasher, no clothes dryer. Watch a movie on a cloudy day? Forget it! If you or a loved one is on life support, or enjoys a Zero Gravity Massage Chair, forget it. Even if you live without a T.V. and use one lamp, YOU WILL RUN OUT OF POWER--so how much rent are you paying for that? Landlords of off the grid rentals will NOT tell you this.

You *will* do your laundry at the Laundromat. Or wait for a sunny day and an overpriced tiny 'off grid' washer. Or you'll cycle many miles to use a 'homemade' washer. Even Americans can go without a clothes dryer, but you most definitely will NOT use one off grid. EVER. (Re-read: Heat Source appliance).

Going out in the evening and want to leave a porch light on? Forget it. Want to leave a lamp on for the dog and it's been raining? Forget it. (Yes, I'm well familiar with LED Headlamps, string lights and solar powered, patio lighting).

Ask yourself: "Do I spend the majority of cloudy days in deep meditation?"
Does my 'to do' list say 'just be'?
Unless you are a complete hermit or seek to live monastically, you are better off going to a Monastery then renting off the grid in northern NM!

Interpreting real estate listing keywords for those new to New Mexico:

"SOLITUDE" = 4wd access on a rough dirt road
"TRANQUILITY = LACK of basic amenities.
"VIEWS" = Nothing nice to say about the house.

Utilities Nearby

"OPEN SPACES" = An over priced place a long way to town.

"ARTIST RETREAT" = I built a crappy house I don't want to live in.

"MAKE YOUR OWN ELECTRICITY" = The equivalent of using a water still in the desert. A few drops after 12 sunny hours.

And this is my favorite: "Be one of the 10% who can see the Milky Way."

Home owners of OFF the grid homes have no business renting out these properties. BEWARE renters! Very few are 'state of the art'. Look at the solar array next to Harry's Road House or SFCC. THAT is what you need. Also if renting an off grid home, it is like having a second job. If it is NOT your own home, you can do nothing to improve conditions of a lackadaisical landlord that simply says 'energy conscientious' or 'energy mindful' is a bunch of BS. We ran out of power while out of town! We weren't even in the house! There's goes the yogurt and the groceries in the fridge.

So you ARE not saving money by living off the grid. In the winter, we unplugged the (small) fridge and put our perishables outside in a cooler. It's like camping only you are paying a $1000 a month.
(Is this the part that makes some people laugh and others angry? Is this the 'rant' part?)

You can camp much cheaper than renting someone else's off the grid shit box. Beware, some of them look pretty nice (especially in fall, summer and sunny days). Remember, "Authentic NM" = LACK OF BASIC AMENITIES.

None of these SOLAR OFF GRID properties are worth

more than $500 a month tops! That is generous, and ONLY WITH an indoor HOT Shower! "Solar Shower Provided"--If that's fine with you--great. Most people renting a property expect hot running water.

Bonus Info: If you are new to New Mexico, understand that you CANNOT drink the water near Madrid/Cerillos. You cannot cook pasta in it either. Forget it.

BONUS Info: "Really nice outhouse" doesn't count as rentable. All the Santa Fe aura in the world will NOT replace a real toilet. Yes, even I can crap in the woods--whilst camping. NOT while paying a lot of rent.

Don't trust anyone telling you Tres Piedras is amazing. (There's no water). If you're going sustainable, you'll need a well.

Test yourself; unplug everything and try it. Keep your printer unplugged too, even if not using it and it's off. It's still sucking power. I think it is definitely worth being aware of your energy usage. We could all learn a few more primitive human skills just beware if you plan to do this full time and PAY A LOT OF RENT. This is what we have learned and I hope it helps you sort out the 'CHARMING CASITAS' of northern NM.

Please note: This is written by someone that does LOVE NM and wishes better things for Santa Fe than having bled out it's entire younger populous and left a town with vacant storefronts. The allure to off the grid is understandable, but it is our experience, you need to OWN your off the grid house to actually have a shot at making the lifestyle work for you.

This post is about RENTING off the Grid and $$: What you are willing to pay for a huge hassle. Buying land and

UTILITIES NEARBY

building? That's up to you. Going vegetarian, dehydrating food, or telling me that a squash lasts a year is not the topic of this post.

There's a reason off the grid owners attempt to rent out these shit boxes to the unsuspecting back to nature sustainable hopeful. They can't sell it because the bank won't cover a mortgage on self-built off grid homes. Most people interested in off the grid, don't have the bucks to buy outright and that would be a huge mistake. Don't let the political climate freak you out. "Trump-apocalypse" could mean going off grid for you. If that's the case, start collecting firewood and learn how to skin a pig, because in the "Trump-apocalypse" even the vegetarians will eat meat again.

Got a good off the grid story? I've heard many from this post and still have YET to hear a positive renting off grid story! (EXCEPT "Sponge-Bathed-All-Winter-Yurt-Man-North-of-Taos"). Hate it or Love this post? I love hearing from everyone! Thanks.

Thank you to recent replies including "Whambulance" "Bewitched by Earthships", "My friend wants to retire off the grid" and "Dude, get over yourself."

ACKNOWLEDGEMENTS

Writing this book has made me a more compassionate human being even though I still cuss sometimes. I've learned what it means to feel at home. It's given me the opportunity to celebrate everything I love about New Mexico and to share that with so many wonderful people. To my surprise, what began as my bummed out exposé on a house outside Santa Fe turned into an amazing conversation. Through this book, I rediscovered a sense of authentic community. Again, I thank everyone who responded to my post.

I am grateful for my husband and best friend, Chris Márquez. Scoring true love in Santa Fe, the worst town in America to find a date, reminds me that great things still happen in Santa Fe. I am also very thankful to Teresa Márquez, the most stylish and literary mother-in-law on earth. Her support and belief in me as a writer daughter-in-law kept me going as I completed this book.

Thank you to the friends that been a part of my life for over a decade since my days working in downtown Santa Fe. Carol, Rebeca, Nikki, Anna, Jeff, you're the ones that know the full story and who I laugh with the most. There are more friends too, new ones and some overseas, Kirsten, Nozipho, Ingrid and Mariana. There are more people than I can mention who really have made a positive impact on my life. It's been a quiet ride for a while as I worked to complete this book. Thank you for being a part of my life and allowing me to be a part of yours.

I'm thankful to my dad for giving me a great sense of humor and because he cracked up laughing when I told him the title of this book. As an avid reader, one who shares my joy of dark humored memoirs, I know he'll enjoy my book.

Several dogs (both young and old) were also instrumental in bringing this book project to fruition. Some have since gone on to rainbow bridge: Junee and Mungo adopted from the Santa Fe Animal Shelter & Humane Society, Princess, Mason, the terrior who lived to be 150 years old and most recently, Lunita Bonita, a great old red heeler who's spirit I will always remember.

Some dogs were at my side the whole time including Bravo and Lily. Beloved dogs, thank you for your patience sitting at my feet. We're going out for a walk now!

I am also thankful for the opportunities to share my writing through Dimestories.org. My friend Jennifer Simpson, host of Dimestories ABQ, showed me that my writing would happily find an audience beyond Craigslist.

ABOUT THE AUTHOR

Jes Márquez is a life long resident of the Land of Enchantment. She lives in New Mexico, currently on the grid. Her favorite things include exploring the human condition, wild places and a dry as sand sense of humor. A dog lover beyond measure, she enjoys working around animals of all kinds. Jes graduated from the University of New Mexico. She plans to be the eccentric author that rolls through town once a month. In her spare time, Jes makes cowboy boots from scratch.

Jes always welcome letters, comments, banter and opportunities. Please write to:

Jes Márquez
P.O. BOX 32664
Santa Fe, NM 87594

email: UtilitiesNearby@gmail.com